Mike —
you're an Urban
Statesman — a true
city leader for
years to come

Sam

THE CEO URBAN STATESMAN

MERCER
UNIVERSITY PRESS

Endowed by
TOM WATSON BROWN
and
THE WATSON-BROWN FOUNDATION, INC.

THE CEO AS
URBAN STATESMAN

SAM A. WILLIAMS

MERCER UNIVERSITY PRESS
MACON, GEORGIA

MUP/ H895

Published by Mercer University Press
© 2014 by Mercer University Press
1400 Coleman Avenue
Macon, Georgia 31207
All rights reserved

9 8 7 6 5 4 3 2 1

Books published by Mercer University Press are printed on acid-free paper that meets the requirements of the American National Standard for Information Sciences— Permanence of Paper for Printed Library Materials.

Library of Congress Cataloging-in-Publication Data

Williams, Sam A.
  The CEO as urban statesman / Sam A. Williams. -- 1st Edition.
    pages cm
  Includes bibliographical references and index.
  ISBN 978-0-88146-510-5 (hardback : alk. paper) -- ISBN 0-88146-510-0 (hardback : alk. paper)
1. Chief executive officers--United States--Case studies. 2. Businesspeople--United States--Case studies. 3. Business and politics--United States--Case studies.
4. Statesmen--United States--Case studies. 5. Cities and towns--United States--Case studies. I. Title.
  HD38.25.U6W55 2014
  322'.30973091732--dc23
                          2014015565

Contents

Introduction   vii

1. The Atlanta Way   1

2. Who Is the Urban Statesman?   14

Defined Case Studies

3. Oklahoma City: A MAP for Change   31

4. Atlanta: Saving Grady   47

5. Salt Lake City: Road Warriors   69

6. Houston: After the Storm   85

7. Columbus, Georgia: Rollin' on the River   99

Best Practices

8. Eight Rules for Successful Urban Statesmanship   133

9. Cautionary Tales   170

Acknowledgments   181

Bibliography   183

Index   189

Introduction

I didn't grow up in an urban environment. My hometown of Obion, Tennessee, today has a population of fewer than 1,200 and has grown since I left for college in 1964. But my years at Georgia Institute of Technology ("Georgia Tech") gave me, in addition to a good education and an electrical engineering degree, an appreciation for the complexities of urban life.

I've lived my post-college life engaged in city-building. I've been involved with the business community of Atlanta since 1971, beginning with the time I spent at Research Atlanta and continuing through my career at Portman Properties, Central Atlanta Progress, and the Metro Atlanta Chamber. Projections suggest that by 2050, 80 percent of the US population will live in an urban environment. That means urban issues will become important to us all.

In my work with the urban business community of Atlanta, I've noticed that politicians are not always the best people to solve a city's public policy problems. On a number of occasions Atlanta's business community has stepped up to solve a problem that challenged the political community, partnering with political interests. Politicians, after all, are committed to the positions they've already staked out and the voters who elected them. Businessmen are not as restrained and can act more independently, building bridges—often behind the scenes. I've labeled the business executives who take action on these public policy issues "urban statesmen," and I think these folks have a really important role.

So what defines an urban statesman? To me, the urban statesman is a business leader who uses business skills to address public sector and community issues. These statesmen focus on both problem solving and advocacy. They define and analyze issues, generate solutions, and often participate in the implementation of the solutions they develop. They become involved because community organizations or governments request their help, or because they discover a problem in the course of their own civic engagement. The effective urban statesman has the resources to gather the necessary talent and information, the negotiating skills to craft an effective answer to an identified problem, and the clout to close the deal.

In addition to describing the characteristics of these "urban statesmen" and the situations in which they are most likely to be successful, I also plan, in this book, to walk through some examples of urban statesmen in action, not only in Atlanta, but in other parts of the country as well. I've provided a variety of examples of urban statesmen at work, so you'll see that this approach to problem solving is applicable to a wide range of situations. Finally I'll draw from those case studies a set of guidelines that should be helpful to the readers of this book, should they decide to become practitioners of urban statesmanship themselves.

Let me add, though, that the case studies examined in this book are by no means the only examples of urban statesmanship out there. They aren't even the only examples I've considered for this study. The Allegheny Conference in Pennsylvania, for instance, has made use of its talented business leaders in a variety of civically oriented public/private partnerships for many years. Denver, Colorado; Minneapolis/St. Paul, Minnesota; Seattle, Washington; and the Greater Cleveland, Ohio, area are virtual hotbeds of urban statesmanship as I have defined it, and they are not the only ones. I have selected these five stories both for their diversity and their similarities, in an attempt to paint as complete a picture as possible of what urban statesmen do and how they do it.

Ultimately, my hope for this book is to provide something of a user's manual for corporate CEOs—those already in leadership positions who want to participate in the civic arena—and for government leaders who would like to enlist the help of the business community. While it seems a given that business executives wishing to operate in the civic arena would be most effective when they are strong leaders, I plan to focus on what distinguishes urban statesmen from other corporate leaders, and, in particular, what enables these business executives to bridge the gap between business and the public sector, engaging politicians and media to resolve public policy issues that are ripe for solution.

1

The Atlanta Way

Working for Ivan Allen, Jr.

My introduction to the world of public policy came when I was a senior in college. As Georgia Tech student body president I discovered that Mayor John Lindsay of New York City had created a city work-study program for college students. His program paid student interns with federal funds given to colleges and universities that agreed to allow students to work in various civic and social organizations. In Atlanta, the federal government was also giving colleges money to hire students as interns, but here the colleges were using the funds only to pay for on-campus jobs. Along with student leaders from other colleges and universities in the Atlanta area, I had a different vision. We wanted to use the funds to pay for internships with civic and social organizations, just as New York did, but the universities said no; they were using the money to pay for students to work as cafeteria workers, as groundskeepers, and in other on-campus capacities, and they saw in this potential reallocation of funds a negative impact to the college budget.

So we organized students from the schools in the city—Emory, Spelman, Morehouse, Georgia State University, and others—and tried to get in to see Mayor Ivan Allen to advocate for our idea. When he wouldn't see us, we did what all students in the 1960s did—we held a demonstration. The first one was really small, but at the second demonstration we had between seventy-five and one hundred students with placards, and we had called the television stations. The mayor sent his Chief Operating Officer, a fellow named George Berry, out in front of City Hall to talk to us, and we were able to get Berry to give us a second meeting.

When we met at City Hall with Berry the second time, Allen walked by and saw us. He came in the room and said to me, "*You* are the young whippersnapper who is stirring up all this stink. Why don't you come in here and help me fix it?" The result was the Atlanta Urban Corps, modeled on Mayor Lindsay's New York City program. Mayor Allen gave us an office at the old Atlanta Municipal Auditorium and some typewriters and a little seed money. Over the next nine months we managed to place five hundred students in internship positions. The city went to the campuses and persuaded them to use the federal work-study money just as John Lindsay had done. The program eventually became a part of Georgia State University, before the federal money dried up and the program went away entirely. I ran the program for eighteen months then headed to Harvard Business School.

Research Atlanta and Action Forum

I first noticed urban statesmen in action when I returned to Atlanta following graduate school as Executive Director of Research Atlanta, a non-profit public policy research organization. Research Atlanta was an outgrowth of an organization called Good Government Atlanta, founded by a group of rising young attorneys and business professionals who shared a desire to improve local public policy-making. Good Government Atlanta grew out of an independent panel of attorneys created by Fifth Circuit Court of Appeals Judge Griffin Bell to investigate crime and its causes, called the Atlanta Commission on Crime and Juvenile Delinquency; funding came from participating law firms, businesses, and foundations.

Our purpose was to provide the "unvarnished facts"—accurately and impartially presented—to policy makers. "If Research Atlanta could present the facts fairly and without partisanship," contended attorney Michael Trotter, one of our founding board members, "we felt solutions could be found to many of our problems. It was therefore essential that Research Atlanta always be correct about its facts. We were very careful and, as a result, we developed a well-deserved reputation for accuracy and fairness."[1]

Much of Research Atlanta's work during my two-year tenure served another new organization, Atlanta Action Forum. Formed in October 1971 in response to the changing political climate as the black community gained power, Action Forum initially comprised a group of sixteen business and community leaders—eight white and eight black—brought together by W.L. "Bill" Calloway, a black real estate executive, and Mills B. Lane, Jr., the white chairman of C&S Bank.[2] Meetings took place monthly on a Saturday morning at the Midnight Sun restaurant, located in architect-developer John Portman's Peachtree Center complex, the only major office complex in Atlanta at the time. "With black political power increasing, and with blacks on the verge of taking over control of city government," Georgia Tech professor Larry Keating argues, "Lane and Calloway wanted black and white business leaders to work together to maintain a strong business influence on city hall."[3] The group met informally with no

---

[1] Michael Trotter, "Research Atlanta: The Early Days" (unpublished paper, Research Atlanta: 1987) 8.

[2] According to Michael Trotter, in addition to Lane and Calloway, the founding members of Action Forum were Coca-Cola president J. Paul Austin, developer Tom Cousins, businessman Lawrence Gellerstedt, architect/developer John Portman, Augustus H. Sterne from Trust Company of Georgia, and Trotter, a lawyer, from the white business community; and bankers Fletcher Coombs and Charles Reynolds, building contractor Herman Russell, insurance executive Jesse Hill, restaurateur James Paschal, businessman John W. Cox, Atlanta Urban League president Lyndon Wade, and city councilman Q.V. Williamson from the black business community. *Atlanta Journal*, in a profile of Calloway, published 11 October 1982, also identifies NAACP president Lonnie King as an original member, although I remember him coming in later, as the school desegregation negotiations developed.

[3] Larry Keating, *Atlanta: Race, Class, and Urban Expansion* (Philadelphia: Temple University Press, 2001) 125.

officers or minutes and no press in attendance, for a frank and open discussion of issues facing the Atlanta community.[4]

Action Forum's birth was well timed. Maynard Jackson, Jr., was then serving as the city's first African-American vice-mayor, and would be elected mayor in 1973. Debates over the creation of the Metropolitan Atlanta Rapid Transit Authority (MARTA) and school desegregation were very much in the news, with strong factions dividing along racial lines. Even so, the seeds of racial cooperation had been planted through the forward-thinking administration of Mayor Ivan Allen, Jr., supported by Coca Cola's Robert Woodruff, and through the work of Dr. Martin Luther King, Jr., and the Southern Christian Leadership Conference.[5] Action Forum provided an important venue for interracial communication.

Because of Research Atlanta's close collaboration with Action Forum, I became the support staff for Action Forum's monthly meetings. From my spot in the corner I watched Atlanta's most impressive urban statesmen in action at a critical time in the city's history. As Bill Calloway, who became a great friend and personal mentor, observed, "The Action Forum was strictly business—the business of making the city work. We recognized that the city would never work with blacks and whites constantly fighting each other rather than working together. We got the people who counted to talk."[6]

---

[4] See, for instance, Clarence Stone, *Regime Politics: Governing Atlanta 1946–1988* (Lawrence: University Press of Kansas, 1989) 97. The structure of the group is also discussed in Ronald H. Bayor, *Race and the Shaping of Twentieth-Century Atlanta* (Chapel Hill: University of North Carolina Press, 1996), and Keating, *Atlanta: Race, Class and Urban Expansion*, cited above.

[5] For more details on the history of racial cooperation (and discord) in Atlanta, I recommend *Where Peachtree Meets Sweet Auburn* (New York: Penguin Books, 1996) by Gary M. Pomerantz, and Frederick Allen's *Atlanta Rising: The Invention of an International City* (Atlanta: Longstreet Press, 1996).

[6] Steve Dougherty, "Kibitzing with Bill Calloway," *Atlanta Journal*, 11 October 1982, 4B.

Michael Trotter, who was one of the initial participants in Action Forum, remembers, "The first meeting [of Action Forum] was an open discussion and survey of many issues facing the city. At that meeting the immediacy of the second MARTA referendum and the seriousness of the situation in the Atlanta Public Schools were identified as problems that needed to be addressed immediately...." Funding for MARTA, Atlanta's mass transit system, was an issue that made the white business community realize the extent of the power of the black middle class, particularly in light of the growing white flight to the suburbs. A 1968 referendum supported mainly by the downtown business community had failed to gain the support of either white suburbanites or the black community. In his analysis of the biracial accommodations that have governed modern Atlanta politics, Clarence Stone, Research Professor of Political Science and Public Policy at Georgia Washington University, notes, "The harsh reality of defeat forced some rethinking, and the small circle of business backers and regional planners who had brought MARTA into being decided they must broaden support and involvement."[7]

With a second referendum scheduled for 1971 approaching, MARTA backers made a special effort to cultivate support in the black community. Following the 1968 referendum, Mayor Ivan Allen had appointed black insurance executive Jesse Hill, president of Atlanta Life Insurance Company and one of the most vocal critics of the first referendum, to the MARTA Board. Hill was also one of the charter members of the newly formed Action Forum, therefore enjoying both a formal position of authority on the board and informal contact with influential white and black community leaders. Hill later told newspaper columnist Maria Saporta, "Many people don't realize how important the Action Forum was.... MARTA would never have made it without the Action Forum."[8]

---

[7] Stone, *Regime Politics*, 99.

[8] Maria Saporta, "Biracial forum changes as city evolves," *Atlanta Journal-Constitution*, 8 December 2003, 6F.

Although the MARTA debate was well underway when Action Forum had its initial meeting in early October 1971, its prompt attention to the issue and the prominence of its members allowed the group to have an impact on the looming referendum.[9] Action Forum co-founder Calloway reported that at the forum's first meeting, "an appropriation was made to the black coalition for work on behalf of MARTA."[10] The funds were used to promote two important additions to the MARTA proposal in the black community: an agreement to "extend affirmative action to MARTA's employment and contracts" and the addition to the proposal of a spur line to the Perry Homes public housing project. Forum member Jesse Hill was instrumental in crafting the changes.[11] "Less than a month after the forum was formed," Saporta reported, "voters in Fulton and DeKalb counties passed the MARTA referendum by the slimmest of margins. The weight of the biracial business community certainly helped tip the vote in MARTA's favor."[12] The referendum failed, however, in predominantly white Cobb and Gwinnett counties.

The School Desegregation Compromise of 1973

I came to Research Atlanta as the MARTA referendum approached, but the issue really heating up at Action Forum in my early days was that of school desegregation. One of my earliest projects was a series of studies, ten reports in all, commissioned by Action Forum dealing with various aspects of Atlanta's public schools. Action Forum had requested these studies as they evaluated how the city should

---

[9] The topics of the early meetings are included in W.L. Calloway's "A Brief History of the Early Days of Atlanta's Action Forum," box 3, folder 14, Michael H. Trotter papers, Y001, Social Change Collection, Special Collections and Archives, Georgia State University, Atlanta, Georgia.

[10] Calloway, "A Brief History of the Early Days of Atlanta's Action Forum," 4.

[11] Stone, *Regime Politics*, 99–100.

[12] Maria Saporta, "Biracial forum changes as city evolves," *Atlanta Journal-Constitution*, 8 December 2003, 6F.

respond to a lawsuit against the Atlanta Public Schools. *Calhoun v. Cook* was initially filed in 1958 by a group of parents supported by the NAACP, which was pushing for metro-wide school desegregation.

School desegregation was not a new issue in Atlanta in 1971. The initial court order requiring Atlanta Public Schools to begin desegregating was issued in 1961, but the process had moved at a glacial pace. At first, the school system employed a sort of "freedom of choice" plan: black students in designated grades who wanted to transfer to majority-white schools participated in a screening process involving interviews with both the students and their parents and a set of scholastic and aptitude tests. The idea was to expand the integrated population by a grade a year. The first year 130 students applied, and nine high-school juniors and seniors were accepted for transfer. The second year, 44 out of 266 applicants, now including tenth-graders, made the cut.[13] One Research Atlanta report quoted an NAACP spokesman as saying, "It's easier to go to Yale than to transfer from one public school to another in Atlanta."[14]

Threatened with more litigation, the school board eased its procedures in 1965, making "freedom of choice" applicable to all grades. By 1970, with "freedom of choice" replaced by a "majority-to-minority transfer" program with mandated transportation assistance, and with school faculties integrated, only 20,000 out of 100,000 students in the Atlanta system were in desegregated schools, and only 34 out of 117 schools were classified as "desegregated"—those enrolling at least 10 percent of each race. Moreover, the school system, which had been 56 percent white in 1961, had by 1971 become 69 percent black as white students deserted the city for the suburban majority-white schools in Cobb and Gwinnett counties.[15] When, in April 1971, the Supreme Court held that massive busing

---

[13] Stone, *Regime Politics*, 103.

[14] Research Atlanta, "School Desegregation in Metro Atlanta 1954–1973," (Atlanta: Atlanta Research, February 1973) 4.

[15] Stone, *Regime Politics*, 10; ibid, 4, 20.

was allowable as a tool for achieving desegregation, the NAACP pursued metro-wide busing as a possible remedy.

On 6 October 1972, the Fifth Circuit Court of Appeals in New Orleans directed that measures be taken "which will desegregate this system *now*" and ordered the school board to submit a comprehensive plan for integration within thirty days. They wanted the system to begin functioning under the new plan by the beginning of its second six-week term, which started November 27.[16]

On October 14, Action Forum met to discuss the lawsuit. The meeting, which I attended as staff support in my capacity as Executive Director of Research Atlanta, took place in the C&S Bank boardroom in downtown Atlanta. Seated at the large round table were thirty of the city's most prominent black and white leaders, including Action Forum members Lonnie King, president of the local chapter of the NAACP, and school board members William Van Landingham and Frank Smith. The featured speaker was US Circuit Court judge Griffin Bell, who had been invited by the group to offer his wisdom on how to bring closure to the integration crisis. Bell, a native of Americus, Georgia, was known for his Southern drawl and sharp wit. Later appointed Attorney General by President Jimmy Carter, he was a legend among the judiciary.

Bell said that while he was not involved with the lawsuit and could not comment on its specifics, he felt that the drawn-out litigation was harmful to the school system and to the community at large. According to my recollection, he said, "I tell litigants who are frustrated by the judicial process to dismiss their attorneys, hold a face-to-face meeting, and make offers toward a negotiated settlement." Those in the room agreed they would talk to those they knew in each group—the local NAACP chapter and the Atlanta

---

[16] Joel L. Fleishman, "The Real Against the Ideal—Making the Solution Fit the Problem: The Atlanta Public School Agreement of 1973," in *Roundtable Justice: Case Studies in Conflict Resolution—Reports to the Ford Foundation*, ed. Robert B. Goldmann (Boulder CO: Westview Press, 1980) 129.

School Board—to see if they might be willing to gather without lawyers present to talk about a compromise solution.

The following Tuesday, NAACP chapter president Lonnie King and Lyndon Wade, executive director of the Atlanta Urban League, along with Bill Van Landingham and Frank Smith for the school board, met and determined that, even though they did not yet know whether a solution was possible, Action Forum's push for a negotiation had potential. They set a second meeting for an enlarged group[17] for October 21. "Within this committee (essentially a replication of the Action Forum coalition)," Clarence Stone reports, "the prevailing view was that Atlanta could not afford the economic consequences of racial turmoil, and biracial agreement was preferable to a decision reached by adversarial procedures."[18]

Not everyone agreed. While I had heard of the Ku Klux Klan, I had never seen firsthand evidence of their operation. During these contentious negotiations, though, one school board representative Bill was threatened and a cross was burned on his lawn.

The factual data on which the discussions were based came from Research Atlanta. Our data made clear that, given the small percentage of whites within the school system in 1972 (22.6 percent), busing within the city of Atlanta would not have resulted in a completely desegregated school system. [19] Local NAACP president Lonnie King captured the problem in an Atlanta Constitution interview: "…[T]here are 80,000 blacks and 20,000 whites in the school system. The white schools are all smaller and the big schools are in the inner city. To split the whites up into groups of ten and send them out to the black schools is just ridiculous. There just aren't enough white folks to go around."[20]

---

[17] For the names of those comprising the committee, see Fleischman, 132.

[18] Stone, *Regime Politics*, 104.

[19] Research Atlanta, "Desegregation," 29.

[20] Junie Brown, "He Catches It From Both Sides," *Atlanta Constitution*, 28 January 1973, B-8.

Somewhat to the surprise of the white committee members, black school board president Dr. Benjamin Mays (who was then also president of Morehouse College) opposed metropolitan-wide busing, as did the biracial committee. The negotiating team considered a variety of scenarios, involving varying levels of required integration within the Atlanta city schools. It was Research Atlanta's job to answer the "What will this do?" question as various proposals were put forward. Research Atlanta supported both sides with facts and figures detailing the racial composition of each school, including a large map reflecting every school's population. Mays later wrote a letter complimenting our factual analysis.

The "Compromise of 1973" proposed by Action Forum, endorsed by the school board, and ultimately approved by the courts, included a student assignment plan requiring each school to have a black enrollment of at least 30 percent, an expanded majority-to-minority transfer program with magnet programs, desegregated school staffs, and, most important to the black community, administrative desegregation, with a specified racial composition for top management including a black superintendent. Concerned, however, about the amount of power vested in the new superintendent, the school board insisted that the chief financial officer and the board's legal counsel be appointed by and report to the board directly, to ensure the board a source of independent information.[21]

Local NAACP president Lonnie King argued that the compromise, which gave blacks control of the administration and staff assignments, would make the system more responsive to the black community; the national NAACP saw it as a sellout,

---

[21] Stone, *Regime Politics*, 104. See also Bayor, *Race and the Shaping of Twentieth-Century Atlanta*, 247; Kevin M. Kruse, *White Flight: Atlanta and the Making of Modern Conservatism* (Princeton NJ: Princeton University Press, 2005) 239.

abandoning integration in exchange for high-level jobs.[22] Ironically, the national chapter sued Atlanta-born King, a major leader in the civil rights movement. After considerable legal wrangling, mostly concerning which lawyers should be in control, the court approved the compromise,[23] effectively settling the long-running lawsuit. In their 4 April 1973 ruling, judges Sydney Smith and Albert Henderson, Jr., wrote:

> Any plan, whether privately conceived, jointly proposed or court imposed, contains features which are objectionable to certain individuals or certain groups.... This plan, at least, appears to the court to satisfy the overwhelming majority of the plaintiff class. On the whole, the plan is deemed fair, adequate, and reasonable.[24]

The national NAACP was less accepting, suspending the Atlanta chapter and removing King from the presidency of the local NAACP chapter because of his support for the compromise.

The Urban Statesman at Work

My work for Action Forum provided for me a window into the world of the business executive as statesman. These men—and in 1971 they were all men because Action Forum did not add its first women members until 1991[25]—were able to use their business expertise and their connections to address issues that stymied politicians, because they were not limited by the necessity of pleasing an electorate to keep their jobs. Bill Calloway put it well: "I work behind closed

---

[22] See Stone and Bayor, cited above, and the excellent article by Fleischman, for more detail on the reaction to the settlement by the NAACP and the Legal Defense Fund, also involved in the negotiation.

[23] Fleischman, 147–73, details the battle between the lawyer representing Lonnie King and, through a power of attorney, eight of the nine plaintiffs in the lawsuit and the lawyers for the NAACP Legal Defense Fund. While his discussion isn't relevant to my point here, it does make interesting reading.

[24] Quoted in Fleischman, 172.

[25] "Action Forum puts out fires on racial issues," *Atlanta Constitution*, 17 October 1991, E1.

doors. You can get more done without a whole lot of publicity. You won't read anything about Bill Calloway, and I don't mind at all."[26] Calloway had earlier told *Atlanta Constitution* reporter Steve Dougherty, "My role has always been in the background. It is true that sometimes you need the sound and the fury to get people's attention. But in order to really effect change, you have to get people to sit down and talk."[27] Because these folks were willing to talk, they were able to solve immense problems. What I witnessed firsthand was the give and take of high-level executives and leaders being very frank about their points of view. They were also willing to compromise for the good of the city. This process was to become known as "The Atlanta Way."

School desegregation was not the last problem Action Forum addressed. The 1974 election of Maynard Jackson, Jr., as Atlanta's first African-American mayor enhanced the role of the Action Forum as a joint voice for the view of the business community in the city. The white business community did not know how to deal with Jackson. He was very confrontational, and he liked to embarrass the white executives. Dan Sweat was president of Central Atlanta Progress at the time, and he and Jackson frequently butted heads. Jackson would refuse to attend a meeting at Trust Company Bank (the very location where the school desegregation compromise had been negotiated), for instance, because he felt the Atlanta banking community did not support his minority contracting goals. White executives needed a way to talk to their black counterparts away from the eyes, and pens, of the media so they could work together to advance business interests, and Action Forum provided that venue.

Over the years, Action Forum considered such issues as affirmative action and minority participation programs, the location of the Atlanta airport, the financing of Underground Atlanta, and

---

[26] Lorri Denise Booker, "Calloway's Action Forum for black-white dialogue bears fruit," *Atlanta Constitution*, 19 June 1988, B1.

[27] Dougherty, "Kibitzing with Bill Calloway," 4B.

repairing the city's sewers.[28] By 2002, when Mayor Shirley Franklin took office, the forum had doubled in size, and its role had changed. "[Franklin's] election and her inclusive style of running the city made it obvious to everybody that we did not need a formally structured, operating Action Forum," said Pete Correll, then-CEO of Georgia-Pacific and co-chair of Action Forum along with former mayor Maynard Jackson. "We all concluded that it should never die, but it shouldn't meet regularly in the climate that Shirley is providing in today's Atlanta."[29] As another Atlanta executive, Jim Balloun, observed, "The Action Forum put itself out of business by being successful."[30]

What made Action Forum so successful? What was it about these executives that made them effective not only at defining and solving problems, but also at implementing the solutions they developed? Those are the questions I have set out to answer.

---

[28] "Action Forum puts out fires on racial issues," E1; and Saporta, "Biracial forum changes as city evolves," 6F.

[29] Saporta, "Biracial forum changes as city evolves," 6F.

[30] Ibid.

2

Who Is the Urban Statesman?

In March 1993, the Frey Foundation, a family foundation based in Grand Rapids, Michigan, published a report examining the ways business executives, CEOs in particular, organized to engage in public sector problem solving. The study examined the ways in which executives worked with public, non-profit, and other institutional leaders to address issues of a civic nature. Focusing on organizations comprising CEO-level participants, the report asked what sorts of issues they most successfully and effectively addressed.[1] In the years since that study was published, at least three additional studies, one by the strategic consulting firm FutureWorks (September 2004), another by the George Washington Institute of Public Policy for the Brookings Institution (September 2006), and an update of the original Frey Foundation study (2011), have examined this issue. All have concluded, as FutureWorks did, that "...metropolitan regions that harness the power of their business community to address common social and economic challenges will be more effective than those that don't."[2] Clearly, business involvement in the public policy arena has the potential to be a good thing.

Even though the Brookings Institution study acknowledges that, "corporate engagement in urban problem solving depends heavily on

---

[1] Frey Foundation, "Taking Care of Civic Business: How Formal CEO-Level Business Leadership Groups Have Influenced Civic Progress in Key American Cities" (March 1993) 8–9.

[2] FutureWorks, "Minding Their Civic Business: A Look at the New Ways Regional Business-Civic Organizations are Making a Difference in Metropolitan North America," (Arlington MA, 2004) 7.

the heads of major firms being actively involved in the civic life of their communities,"[3] all of these studies address the issue of business involvement in civic affairs on an organizational level. All focus on engagement in the public policy arena at the point of what FutureWorks calls the "business-civic organization," a term that includes such organizations as chambers of commerce, corporate leadership organizations limited to CEOs, and bridge organizations that combine the top executives of private, non-profit, institutional, and government organizations. None of these studies addresses the involvement of the individual CEO in the public policy process.

The Urban Statesman Defined

Bear with me while I repeat a definition: the person I have come to call the "urban statesman" is a corporate leader who uses business skills to address and solve public sector and community issues. These men and women focus on both problem solving and advocacy, defining and analyzing issues, generating solutions, and often participating in the implementation of the solutions they develop. The problems that receive their attention may come to them as requests for help from community organizations or government, or as the result of observation from their own civic engagement. These leaders do not operate in a vacuum; they often engage the help of sponsors or other interested parties (sometimes even opponents) who are seeking solutions to the same civic problems. The effective urban statesman has access to the resources and support organizations to gather the necessary talent and information, the analytical and negotiating skills to craft an effective answer to an identified problem, and the clout to close the deal.

---

[3] George Washington Institute of Public Policy, "Corporate Citizenship and Urban Problem Solving: The Changing Civic Role of Business Leaders in American Cities," (Brookings Institution Metropolitan Policy Program, September 2006) 10.

How does the interested CEO best approach these tasks? What characteristics make for the most effective urban statesman? In the literature of business management, leadership development, and the social responsibility of business, there is very little written about how to initiate and maintain civic involvement effectively. So, while I have spent time with the literature of business as I attempt to answer these questions, I have found it more productive to talk with my colleagues—the executive directors, presidents, and other executives of the business-civic organizations that engage in public policy work—and to ask them to identify the characteristics of their most effective individual performers in the policy arena. I've also talked to some of the leaders they have identified. Having spent 45 years working in the Atlanta business community, I feel uniquely positioned to develop a profile of the urban statesman though a combination of literature, conversation, and observation.

Doing Good While Doing Well

Economic development consultant Rob Radcliff, managing principal with Resource Development Group in Columbus, Ohio, says urban statesmen are driven by a combination of enlightened self-interest and altruism. Passionately committed to their business enterprises, these statesmen are also, and sometimes equally, committed to the place or the issue in which they choose to be involved. [4] As Adam Grant says in his 2013 book, *Give and Take,* these business executives seek to "add value" to the communities in which they operate.[5] They have "a deep interest in their communities and a deep desire to serve," observes Maureen McDonald, former Executive Director of the Denver Metro Leadership Foundation. "They think in terms of community, and they see themselves as community leaders. They take a more holistic approach."[6]

---

[4] Rob Radcliff, interview, 5 July 2011.
[5] Adam Grant, *Give and Take* (New York: Viking Press, 2013) 55.
[6] Maureen McDonald, interview, 21 December 2011.

But self-interest is part of the picture as well. A business's image can benefit from local involvement, which is the reason companies frequently call attention to their community service activities. Mick Fleming, president of American Chamber of Commerce Executives, observes that acting to improve one's community helps "make the place attractive to talent and investment," both of which are good for one's business. Willingness to engage can also serve as an "insurance policy." Fleming says, "If you are involved in the community, you may not be blindsided by the local media or left to fight an unfriendly regulation or legislative proposal on your own."[7]

Urban statesmanship, though, is a bit different from chairing the local symphony board or heading up the United Way campaign, as important as those things are to a community. Those tasks are not controversial; the policy world is different. Radcliff observes that the urban statesman requires a certain amount of organizational courage; executives must be "willing to go against standard conservative political sensibilities, plant a flag in the sand, and put time and company resources behind their efforts."[8]

This is no small demand, and it affects what executives are willing to do. A.D. "Pete" Correll, one of Atlanta's premier urban statesmen (you'll meet him when we get to the case study portion of this discussion), had retired as chairman and CEO of Georgia-Pacific and was heading up a private equity firm when he took on the reorganization of Grady Hospital in 2007. "I could never have done this while I was running Georgia-Pacific," he says now. "The first time pickets showed up at a Wal-Mart or some other place that sold our products I would have been in big trouble with my board and my stockholders. You have to be really careful with racial or hot political issues or faith and values issues—they are really hard to handle. Since I ran a private equity business no one really cared what I did,

---

[7] Mick Fleming, interview, 22 June 2011.
[8] Rob Radcliff, interview, 5 July 2011.

but for an executive in a public company, controversy is difficult."[9] Keith Rattie, a Salt Lake City urban statesman who served as chairman of Questar, the second largest stockholder-owned corporation in Utah, and its spinoff, QEP Resources, shares this view. One of the first questions he asks himself in deciding whether to become involved in a public policy issue, he says, is: "Is this something I could stand in front of institutional investors and defend?"[10]

A Sense of Place

Our CEO urban statesman typically receives a level of respect from his or her peers based partly on business success (doing well), but more importantly on voluntary public leadership (doing good). CEOs generally don't cross the line into urban statesmanship just because of a desire to "do good" in a general sense, however. Most of them have a passionate connection either to their community or to a particular issue. Douglas Henton, John Melville, and Kim Walesh, in their book, *Civic Revolutionaries*, call this commitment to community "stewardship of place." Companies are willing for their CEOs to become "stewards of place," they argue, "because they recognize that their long-term prosperity is tied to the prosperity of their community."[11] Because an area's economic success depends on attracting and retaining entrepreneurial, technical, and creative people, and because such people are mobile, have many choices, and have become "sophisticated consumers of place," Henton *et al* continue, a positive community quality of life is a competitive asset.[12]

---

[9] Pete Correll, interview, 28 November 2011.

[10] Keith Rattie, interview, 9 April 2012.

[11] Douglas Henton, John Melville, and Kim Walesh, *Civic Revolutionaries: Igniting the Passion for Change in America's Communities* (San Francisco: Jossey-Bass, 2004) 96.

[12] Ibid., 143.

The most effective urban statesmen are often closely tied to place; those who do not have strong personal ties to their location tend to operate in a context where community involvement is a strong cultural value of the business community. Roy Williams, president of the Greater Oklahoma City Chamber, describes his city as a place where both of the these conditions hold, and provides one of the best examples of urban statesmanship in the MAPS (Metropolitan Area Projects) capital improvement program you will read about later. "Most of Oklahoma City's executives are homegrown," says Williams:

> Devon Energy, Chesapeake Energy, Sandridge Energy, Sonic, Love's all are headquartered here. The Oklahoma Gas and Electric executive is from New York, and the AT&T and Cox Communications executives transferred in, but within months they were drinking the water. We tell Chamber leadership to reach out and bring them in. Continental Resources from Enid, Oklahoma, [moved] here in March [2012] and we've [worked] with them so they [would] be engaged by the time they [moved]. Boeing, Dell, and Quad Graphic from Milwaukee, all say no one tried to draw them in where they were before, but we did.... [The result is that] we have created a culture where what we can dream, we can do.[13]

It should come as no surprise, then, that places where local business culture is less supportive of civic participation experience less involvement. Mick Fleming notes that civic involvement of business executives varies across the country. It can be especially difficult to organize corporate leaders around civic goals in parts of the Northeast, where executives are less likely to live where they work. Fleming says, "For instance, executives often run businesses in New York City but live in Stamford, Connecticut, but some reverse that commute. Either way, it makes community engagement tough." In mega-metropolitan regions, such as those in the Boston-Washington corridor or southern California, competition among

---

[13] Roy Williams, interview, 28 July 2011.

organizations and causes is everywhere. He continues: "In such sprawling, populous locales, business leaders sometimes remain largely anonymous rather than connecting to neighbors."[14] While corporate celebrities such as Warren Buffett and Bill Gates can make a major impact with large philanthropic gifts, Fleming notes that, "such transformational gifts are marginally, if at all, related to the communities in which they or their companies reside."[15]

An increase in restructuring and consolidation within certain industries (banking and utilities, for example) and the globalization of business also raise red flags for some observers about the future of CEO involvement in civic issues. The Brookings Institution, for example, has observed that, "the gain or loss of major banks and other financial institutions has had an effect both on financial contributions to civic causes and, perhaps even more important, the leadership of the corporate community. Declining employment in manufacturing has led to the demise or relocation of major firms, and with them the loss of prominent CEOs. Furthermore, business demands on executives of newer, fast-growing manufacturing firms appear to leave them little time for civic activities."[16] They conclude: "Regardless of whether they gained or lost large companies, many regions now have fewer top executives among whom to spread civic work, and those executives often lack either the interest or experience in civic affairs."[17]

The Frey Foundation in their most recent study, "The New Landscape of Civic Business," while acknowledging that "CEOs who are native to [a] region are more likely to have greater loyalty and

---

[14] Mick Fleming, interview, 22 June 2011.

[15] Ibid.

[16] George Washington Institute of Public Policy, "Corporate Citizenship and Urban Problem Solving," 10.

[17] Ibid., 14.

involvement in civic efforts,"[18] also quotes Jeff Finkle of the International Economic Development Council, who questions whether CEOs will continue to be interested in civic service agendas. Finkle explains: "There are still homegrown businesses where the entrepreneur is at the helm, with ties to the community, and they will engage, fund, exercise their civic pride, and will gladly participate in private sector-led civic projects. However, a growing number of corporate CEOs are unwilling to play, and if it is not a headquarters community, it is more difficult to get them engaged. Their focus is on producing to the bottom line. They have no civic leadership 'skill,' per se, and there are no rewards within the corporate structure for participating, so many corporate CEOs walk away from civic initiatives."[19]

My experience in Atlanta reinforces these observations. In my early days, I observed Mills B. Lane, founder and chairman of C&S Bank, and architect/developer John C. Portman, making decisions without the worry of oversight from a board of directors or shareholders from outside the community. Today's more global companies have tended to gobble up medium-sized firms into national businesses with fewer "hometown" ties. Additionally, the Atlanta president of a national bank who was a top leader in the Metro Atlanta Chamber told me that he had to be careful as a civic leader. If he did great deeds and was publicly celebrated for them it could be helpful to his career, but if the media criticized him for taking an unpopular position, it could hurt his career climb inside the bank.

In the current global economy, both corporations and their executives seem to have lost their sense of geographic connection. Companies encourage their executives to remain both mobile and

---

[18] Frey Foundation, "The New Landscape of Civic Business: How Business Leadership is Influencing Civic Progress in Our Metropolitan Regions Today," (2012) 2.

[19] Ibid., 17.

focused on the bottom line, and executive jobs are more tenuous. A 2012 report by The Conference Board sets the average tenure of S&P 500 CEOs at 8.4 years, down from 10 years in 2000, and attributes the change to both a greater willingness of corporate directors to dismiss an underperforming executive and "voluntarily shorter tenures" in response to the pressures of an increasingly competitive global marketplace. [20] This combination of corporate loss of connection to a particular locale and executive transience, says Robert H. McNulty, president of Partners for Livable Communities, makes business-based civic leadership harder to find. He asks: "How do you create a civic connection and a desire to serve in a foot-loose corporation?"[21]

The key, according to past US Chamber of Commerce and Metro Atlanta Chamber chair and current Atlanta urban statesman Tom Bell, is company culture: "As companies become more global, there's less focus on the executives' home communities. I think if a company creates the expectation of a civic or community obligation younger executives will do it and like it. There's a lot of satisfaction in helping your community. But if companies don't create the expectation they won't [participate]."[22] And even in the face of this increased executive disconnect, places with a culture of civic commitment (such as Oklahoma City, mentioned above) continue to grow urban statesmen. Atlanta's business community is well known for engaging new CEOs in civic endeavors. Business success is measured by the degree to which a CEO gives back to the community in leadership efforts as well as by his or her financial impact.

I've also noticed that a certain civic confidence appears where the business community has successfully involved itself in a public policy endeavor, leading to the likelihood that the pattern will be repeated. I

---

[20] "Average Tenure of CEOs Declined to 8.4 Years, The Conference Board Reports," http://www.conference-board.org/press/presssdetail.cfm?press-id=4453, accessed 14 March 2013.

[21] Robert H. (Bob) McNulty, interview, 30 June 2011.

[22] Tom Bell, interview, 2 December 2011.

don't think it is a coincidence that two of our case-study cities—Salt Lake City and Atlanta—had successfully hosted the Olympic Games, or that Columbus, Georgia's, whitewater project followed a long pattern of successful business engagement with quality-of-life issues. For all its pessimism on this front, the Brookings Institution agrees: "Where business leaders have created organizations and networks that can mobilize economic resources and talent to influence public policy or economic activity, they are more likely to find satisfaction in civic engagement, in turn reinforcing their commitments."[23]

In addition to having a vested interest in making a specific community better, effective urban statesmen tend to look beyond business-specific issues to the big picture, maintaining a long-term vision that connects community quality-of-life issues to their business interests, says Tom DiFiore, president of National Community Development Services, a community and economic development fund-raising firm based in Atlanta.[24] They exhibit what Henton, Melville, and Walesh call "visionary pragmatism," facing "the tension between vision and reality" by employing "a set of core values that allow leaders to make realistic choices among many good ideas and then persevere in the face of challenges."[25] They "build a convincing case for change in their communities—accumulating information, ideas and allies in the process. They diagnose the challenges facing their communities, the tensions between competing values that must be addressed in new ways. They creatively describe, reframe, measure, and connect issues and root causes. They try to understand what is working, what is not working, and what might work."[26] (We'll talk about all these practices—extensive fact-finding, development of alternatives, building consensus, developing action

---

[23] George Washington Institute of Public Policy, "Corporate Citizenship and Urban Problem Solving," 11.

[24] Tom DiFiore, interview, 6 July 2011.

[25] Henton, Melville, and Walesh, *Civic Revolutionaries*, 204.

[26] Ibid., 238.

plans—later when we examine the best practices of successful urban statesmen.) Having laid such a foundation, Harvard professor Bill George argues, effective leaders will then "convey such a sense of passion for their purpose that people share it and feel inspired by the mission."[27]

This visionary focus and persuasive appeal inspire Ray Ackerman's dedication to the Bricktown Canal in Oklahoma City; the involvement of Tom Bell, Pete Correll, and Michael Russell in the Grady Hospital restructuring in Atlanta; and the wholesale commitment of Scott Anderson, Keith Rattie, Clark Ivory, and Lane Beattie to the 2006 transportation referendum in Salt Lake City as you will read later on.

Boundary Crossing

Urban statesmen from the business community seem to be particularly effectivé in situations that require the crossing of political, geographic, racial, or organizational boundaries. The Alliance for Regional Stewardship sees these statesmen as "regional stewards," and notes, "they reach across jurisdictional, organizational, ethnic, and other boundaries to seek solutions to community problems. They are not deterred by turf issues. In fact, it is striking how often regional stewards are building collaborative solutions outside the traditional government structures."[28] The effective urban statesman is "not parochial," Maureen McDonald says,[29] and Tom DiFiore concurs. "They don't see boundaries," he notes, but instead are willing to move across geographic and political borders to get things done.[30]

---

[27] Bill George, *True North: Discovering Your Authentic Leadership* (New York: John Wiley & Sons, 2007) 164.

[28] Alliance for Regional Stewardship, *Regional Stewardship: A Commitment to Place Monograph*, series 1 (Palo Alto CA: Alliance for Regional Stewardship, 2000) 11.

[29] Maureen McDonald, interview, 21 December 2011.

[30] Tom DiFiore, interview, 6 July 2011.

Business executives can be effective in boundary-bridging situations because they are NOT politicians who have responsibilities to geographically or jurisdictionally bound constituencies. Not limited to representing the interests of a particular group, business-based statesmen are able to gather information and develop solutions to problems that reflect and balance the interests of all stakeholders. When issues seem ripe for solution, they can gather together potential partners, consultants, and sponsors from various political and geographic jurisdictions without the risk of irritating or ignoring constituents. These are common business approaches to problem solving, and the most effective urban statesmen are quite good at them. You'll see boundary crossing at work later when we look at the work of a disaster relief task force in Houston, Texas, the Grady Hospital restructuring in Atlanta, and Columbus, Georgia's whitewater project.

An additional factor differentiating these urban statesmen from political leaders is their tendency to stay in the background. Like Bill Calloway of Atlanta Action Forum, they "work behind closed doors."[31] They function as what Adam Grant calls "givers," taking care to recognize the contributions of others to their efforts.[32] It's not often you see the name of one of these statesmen in the papers or on the evening news, and when you do, they are often quick to give credit to the political leaders with whom they work in their public-private partnerships. There's a good reason for this behavior, as Rick Stafford, former CEO of the Allegheny Conference and current Carnegie Mellon University professor, observes: "Political leaders want and need credit for what they do. As a politician you can't be effective unless people think you are. It's part of the job. There's not

---

[31] Lorri Denise Booker, "Calloway's Action Forum for black-white dialogue bears fruit," *Atlanta Constitution*, 19 June 1988, B1.

[32] Grant, *Give and Take*, 84.

much 'I couldn't have done it without you' in them. The urban statesman has to understand this and be willing to accommodate."[33]

Political Acumen

While urban statesmen are not politicians, however, the best of them possess a good deal of political acumen. Former Pittsburgh mayor Tom Murphy, now a Senior Resident Fellow with the Urban Land Institute, observes that public-private partnerships can be a challenge for business people because the public and private sectors have very different cultures: "Business is hierarchical; the public sector is more chaotic because it is democratic."[34] Effective urban statesmen recognize the differences between the world of business and the public policy culture, and they adapt. Tom Bell, reflecting on his own experience moving into the public policy world, opines, "Business people working in public policy often think they can deal with people like they do in their companies, but they can't. The only way to make things work is to build a community around an idea; you can't order it done. You have to invest in selling the process; you have to be willing to listen, even to bad ideas, and to take two steps forward and one step back." [35]

Like the best politicians the urban statesman at his or her best knows how to build coalitions, develop consensus, and work the

---

[33] Rick Stafford, interview, 13 January 2012.

[34] Tom Murphy, interview, 9 November 2011.

[35] Tom Bell, interview, 2 December 2011. Ronald A. Heifetz, Alexander Grashow, and Marty Linsky, in *The Practice of Adaptive Leadership: Tools and Tactics for Changing Your Organization and the World* (Boston: Harvard Business Publishing, 2009) 133, define "acting politically" as "using your awareness of the limits of your own authority, and of stakeholders' interests, as well as power and influence networks in your organization, to forge alliances with people who will support your efforts, to integrate and defuse opposition, and to give valuable dissenting voices a hearing as you adjust your perspective, interventions and mobilize adaptive work." Their definition is more academic, but makes the same points.

power structures of both the business and political communities to get things done. These business executives possess the boundary-crossing skills identified by the late John W. Gardner in his classic work *On Leadership*: agreement building (conflict resolution, mediation, compromise, and coalition building, networking, exercising power that comes from one's personal character rather than from one's office), institution building (constructing problem-solving systems and choosing leaders to preside over them), and flexibility.[36] Tom DiFiore calls this a "stewardship of authority." He notes, "[Such leaders] recognize and appreciate the clout they wield, and feel they have a responsibility [to use this power] that goes beyond their shareholders."[37]

Good in a Crisis

Finally, effective urban statesmen work best with short-term timelines, not multi-year commitments. They make their best contributions in high-pressure, urgent crisis-like situations, the type of situations Malcolm Gladwell calls a "tipping point," and that former Intel CEO Andrew Grove labels a "strategic inflection point." Gladwell defines a tipping point, a term he borrows from epidemiology, as "the name given to that moment in an epidemic when a virus reaches critical mass. It's the boiling point. It's the moment on the graph when the line starts to shoot straight upwards."[38] In extending the term beyond its epidemiological use, Gladwell calls it "the moment of critical mass, the threshold, the boiling point."[39] Grove defines the same concept in a business context, noting "...[A] strategic inflection point is when the balance of

---

[36] John W. Gardner, *On Leadership* (New York: Free Press, 1990) 119ff.

[37] Tom DiFiore, interview, 6 July 2011.

[38] Malcolm Gladwell, "The Tipping Point," http://www.gladwell.com/the-tipping-point/, accessed 6 September 2012.

[39] Malcolm Gladwell, *The Tipping Point: How Little Things Can Make a Big Difference* (Boston: Little, Brown and Company, 2000) 12.

forces shifts from the old structure, from the old ways of doing business and the old ways of competing, to the new."[40] When we ignore a tipping point we risk either failure or loss of opportunity. In short, either we react or negative consequences ensue.

The urgency inherent in such a critical point can create a persuasive need for action. Times when major change is critical provide opportunities for urban statesmen to work effectively, Bob McNulty says, because such scenarios "push the public sector to seek help and business to step up."[41] Boundary issues tend to disappear, and the critical question becomes who has the necessary skills and vision to solve the problem. In such instances, Scott Anderson, president and CEO of Zions Bank in Salt Lake City and a major player in the Salt Lake County transportation referendum in 2006, observes, "the business approach—how you analyze and synthesize data, how you make things work from an economic point of view (cost/benefit analysis) is really valuable."[42] In addition, Atlantan Tom Bell adds, "Business people bring the gift of experience, insight and implementation skills. Most public sector people have political skills, but not necessarily the executive, problem-solving, and management skills that business people have developed."[43] Suddenly all of those fact-finding, alternative-developing, and action-plan-constructing skills become quite important.

The type of issues over which such urgency arises varies from community to community, as you will see in the case studies that

---

[40] Andrew S. Grove, *Only the Paranoid Survive: How to Exploit the Crisis Points that Challenge Every Company and Career* (New York: Doubleday, 1996) 33. Grove also offers a more explicit mathematical definition: "Mathematically, we counter an inflection point when the rate of change of the slope of the curve (referred to as its 'second derivative') changes sign, for instance, going from negative to positive. In physical terms, it's where a curve changes from convex to concave, or vice versa" (32).

[41] Bob McNulty, interview, 30 June 2011.

[42] Scott Anderson, interview, 6 April 2012.

[43] Tom Bell, interview, 2 December 2011.

follow. The Frey Foundation's original 1993 study argued that "brick and mortar" and infrastructure projects make for good private-public partnerships.[44] Their 2011 follow-up study further notes, "…[T]wo issues [that] surfaced as concerns of civic business organization practitioners [were] transportation and infrastructure and public education."[45] The Oklahoma City and Salt Lake City case studies you will read shortly confirm that. Maureen McDonald and Bob McNulty see particular opportunity in problems that cross political boundaries, which you'll see in the Atlanta and Houston case studies. In all of the studies that follow, though, you will see executives who combine doing well with doing good, have a strong sense of place and a commitment to the issue at hand, are willing to do a job without demanding the lion's share of the credit, have a good sense of how to use their power in the political as well as the business arena, and perform well in a crisis.

One last important point I'd like to make about the nature of the urban statesmen is that he or she is NEVER a Lone Ranger. The urban statesman sees the variety of resources necessary to address a problem, accurately accesses what he or she brings to the table, and then searches for individuals or organizations that can fill the gaps. Otis White, president of Civic Strategies, Inc., an Atlanta-based strategic planning firm that works with cities and civic organizations, notes: "Civic projects are typically played out in three dimensions: a political dimension (where the project runs a gauntlet of political approvals), a financial dimension (where it raises money), and a public dimension (where citizens must feel assured this is the right thing to do at this time). You don't often find people who can work in all these dimensions, so you have to build a team that can."[46] Urban statesmen are acutely aware of this need for "a combination of

---

[44] Frey Foundation, "Taking Care of Civic Business," 36.
[45] Frey Foundation, "The New Landscape of Civic Business," 3.
[46] Otis White, *The Great Project* (Apple iBook, 2012) 31.

talents"[47] and are eager to work with others to help their projects succeed. At the end of the day, one might hear, "we couldn't have done it without her," but never "he did it all by himself."

Let's look now at the urban statesman in action.

---

[47] Ibid., 11.

3

Oklahoma City: A MAP for Change

Oklahoma City calls Ray Ackerman "Old Man River" for a reason. The Oklahoma River, over which a recently dedicated statue of Ackerman presides, is a far cry from the dry, dusty channel of the North Canadian River that the city had known since its inception. Ackerman's leadership, combined with that of former mayor Ron Norick, explains the difference.

Dry and Dusty

In the mid-1980s, Oklahoma City was a city treading water. The failure of a local bank in July 1981, followed by an oil bust, had slowed or cancelled a number of planned improvements to the downtown area; the financial disaster of the 1984 New Orleans World's Fair cast a pall on plans for a similar fair to celebrate Oklahoma City's Centennial in 1989;[1] and the city had competed and lost in the battle to bring new industry—something other than natural gas and oil—to the area. The misfires included an American Airlines maintenance facility and a Defense Finance Accounting Center.[2]

In 1990, Oklahoma City was one of 94 of cities competing for a United Airlines maintenance facility. To lure the company, the city collaborated with the state legislature to create an economic incentive package that included sales tax exemptions for computer sales, materials brought into Oklahoma for construction, and spare parts needed for airplane maintenance. A countywide sales tax expected to generate as much as $160 million toward plant construction, with

---

[1] Steve Lackmeyer and Jack Money, *OKC: Second Time Around* (Oklahoma City OK: Full Circle Press, 2006) 76–78.
[2] Lackmeyer and Money, *OKC*, 107.

airport bonds financing the remainder of the construction costs. Oklahoma City made it to the final three in the competition, but ultimately lost the facility to Indianapolis.[3]

Oklahoma City's mayor at the time was Ron Norick, the president of a family-owned printing company who was elected mayor in 1987 running on an economic development platform. Normally, I would not include a mayor in the "urban statesman" category, but Oklahoma City uses a city manager form of government; its mayor in the 1990s made less than $2,000 a year and kept his day job. I consider Norick a businessman who made an extraordinary gift of his time to his city.

Norick was distressed by the loss of the maintenance facility. Why, he wondered, did Oklahoma City keep coming up short in the competition for new business? When he looked at his own city, reporters Steve Lackmeyer and Jack Money contend, "...the mayor saw an aging convention center and a baseball stadium so ancient it could have been uncovered by an archaeological dig." [4] The World Championship Quarter Horse Show, long a fixture at the state fair grounds, was threatening to leave "...in large part due to deteriorating horse barns without modern amenities found in other regional cities."[5] The economy was barely pumping enough sales tax into the city government to keep it operating, providing no opportunity for expansion or improvement of city facilities. The city was at a critical juncture. "In 1992, Oklahoma City was not simply failing in its efforts to move ahead," said Lackmeyer and Money. "Norick feared it was falling behind."[6]

This view was reinforced by Ray Ackerman, head of the Oklahoma City-based advertising agency Ackerman McQueen and

---

[3] Lackmeyer and Money, *OKC*, 106–7.

[4] Lackmeyer and Money, *OKC*, 107.

[5] John Parker, "MAP to the Future: Norick Feeling Easy Down Final Stretch," *Daily Oklahoman*, 12 December 1993, News, 1, http://infoweb.newsbank.com/iw-search/we/InfoWeb.

[6] Lackmeyer and Money, *OKC*, 107.

incoming chairman of the Chamber of Commerce. At a 1990 Chamber retreat, Ackerman had reported the results of a recent survey: a substantial majority of Oklahoma City residents had a negative view of their hometown. Lackmeyer and Money summarized: "When asking people what they thought was good about the community, Ackerman's surveyors repeatedly heard it possessed a good quality of life, good weather, that it was a great place to raise a family, was easy to get around, and had plenty of recreational opportunities. Even so, an astounding 65 percent of those surveyed still told questioners they did not think Oklahoma City was a good place to live."[7] Based on the survey, Ackerman concluded, "No one liked what they saw and there was no plan for anything better in the future."[8] Nationally, Ackerman reported, Oklahoma City's image was that of "a dry and dusty hick town in an oil and gas setting, complete with cowboys and Indians."[9]

Norick visited Indianapolis and other cities to see what they had that Oklahoma City lacked. Lackmeyer and Money reported: "Norick drove through downtown Indianapolis, stopping to stroll along a little recreational canal built in the heart of the city. He saw a vibrant district with new restaurants and hotels. A statue standing in the middle of a traffic circle caught [his] attention. Downtown Indianapolis with its renovated buildings stunned Norick. There were a lot of things going on."[10] By contrast, nothing was happening in Oklahoma City.

The mayor concluded that United Airlines had made a "quality of life" decision: Indianapolis was a vibrant city, and Oklahoma City

---

[7] Lackmeyer and Money, *OKC*, 110.

[8] Bob Burke with Joan Gilmore, *Old Man River: The Life of Ray Ackerman* (Oklahoma City: Oklahoma Heritage Association, 2002) 251.

[9] Tim Chavez, "Watering Down Divisions Chamber Leader Sees River Revival as Key to Unifying City," *Daily Oklahoman*, 2 December 1990, Business, 1.

[10] Lackmeyer and Money, *OKC*, 112, based on interview with Norick.

was not.[11] Roy Williams, current CEO of the Greater Oklahoma City Chamber of Commerce recalled, "[United's decision] was a hammer in the forehead. It made our leadership take a real look at this community and reassess ourselves."[12] "United taught us one thing," Norick said at a 1992 press conference. "In order to compete effectively, we have to look like a big-league city. When it comes right down to it, Oklahoma City is still not considered a big league city."[13]

Old Man River

Ackerman chose to tackle the problem of Oklahoma City's image at an October 1990 Chamber of Commerce board of directors' retreat in Shawnee, Oklahoma. His goal was to convince the Chamber leaders to create a visionary plan to be completed over a number of years, designed to turn Oklahoma City into a truly great national city. A number of suggestions were offered: indoor and outdoor sports facilities, a new library and learning center, hotels, fairground improvements, renovations to the civic center music hall (a favorite of the mayor), and a light rail or trolley system for downtown transportation. Ackerman's particular favorite was a proposal to dam the North Canadian River, creating a recreational area, combined with a canal connecting the river with downtown and creating an entertainment district similar to San Antonio's River Walk.[14]

Ackerman had been drawn to rivers since his boyhood days in Pittsburgh, but the North Canadian in Oklahoma City bore little resemblance to the Ohio, Allegheny, or Monongahela of his youth.

---

[11] Brett Rosenberg, "Oklahoma City: A Win-Win," *U.S. Mayor Newspaper*, 77.11 (28 June 2010): 21, http://www/usmayors.org/usmayorsnewspaper/documents/06_28_10_/pg 21_OKC_win_win.asp.

[12] Douglas Henton, John Melville, and Kim Walesh, *Civic Revolutionaries: Igniting the Passion for Change in America's Communities* (San Francisco: Jossey-Bass, 2004) 213.

[13] Parker, "MAP to the Future: Norick Feeling Easy Down Final Stretch," 12 December 1993, News 1.

[14] Burke, *Old Man River*, 250–51.

During Oklahoma City's early years, the river was either dry or ran at a trickle, except in the spring when it was the source of destructive floods. In the early 1900s, the river area was a popular gathering spot, home to the Delmar Gardens amusement park, the largest amusement park west of St. Louis, Missouri, at the time, as well as baseball fields, a zoo, and walking and hiking trails. But spring flooding brought destruction and hoards of mosquitoes, forcing the park to close and the zoo and ball fields to relocate in 1910.[15]

In 1923, after the river flooded downtown, the city's leaders convinced the Army Corps of Engineers to straighten the river, remove the trees and shrubs that lined its banks, and dredge rock and sand from the river bottom to create tall berms along the banks for flood control.[16] The result was what Pat Downes, general manager of the Oklahoma City Riverfront Redevelopment Authority later described as "America's ugliest river."[17] The local joke that the North Canadian River was "the only river in the world that is mowed three times a year" was based on fact.[18]

Ackerman was not the first person to see the potential of the North Canadian River. In Oklahoma City's earliest days, founding fathers Henry Overholser and Charles G. "Gristmill" Jones needed a source of power for a proposed flour mill. They convinced the townspeople to invest in the Oklahoma City Ditch and Water Power Company, which built a six-mile canal with solid banks to divert the river flow and provide water power for the mill. Unfortunately the plan was a colossal failure. Historian Bob Blackburn reported, "When the canal was completed, they opened the gates and water flowed down the channel. The first day, there were celebrations. The second day, the water level dropped and, finally, within a few days, the

---

[15] Burke, *Old Man River*, 245.

[16] Burke, *Old Man River*, 245–46.

[17] John Parker, "Channel at Center of Plan," *Daily Oklahoman*, 28 November 1993, News, 22.

[18] Burke, *Old Man River*, 244.

water disappeared."[19] The water had been absorbed by the sandy bottom. Attempts to shore up the canal bed with timbering were not successful, and the project was abandoned in 1892.

In more recent times, a redevelopment proposal by I.M. Pei in the 1960s, an update to Pei's proposal called the Gruen Central City Plan in 1974, and a 1980's plan known as "String of Pearls" (supported by Ackerman) had also focused on turning the river into an asset. While Pei's plan treated the river as merely a bit of scenic flood control, the later versions envisioned a series of dams used to create a string of lakes bordered by recreational opportunities like the zoo and the walking and hiking trails of the old days, retail development, and restaurants.[20]

Still, there was concern that the fiasco of the 1890s might be repeated. Ackerman turned to the Oklahoma City Riverfront Redevelopment Authority, created to look at the development of the river, and pushed them to conduct a feasibility study to determine whether the riverbed would hold water and if a filled river would pose a flooding hazard to the downtown area. The 1990 study, conducted by the engineering firm RGDC, concluded that it was feasible to build dams and impound water along the river. That information was in Ray Ackerman's hands at the Shawnee retreat.[21]

Crafting a Vision

Shaped by Ackerman's leadership, a new plan for Oklahoma City, called "Visions for a New Frontier," emerged from the Chamber retreat. The plan had as its centerpiece bringing the North Canadian River into downtown Oklahoma City by building a canal from the river into the city.[22] Ackerman saw the river as a venue for a wide

---

[19] Bob Blackburn, *Heart of the Promised Land: An Illustrated History* (Oklahoma City OK: Windsor Publications, 1982) 69.

[20] Lackmeyer and Money, *OKC*, 120–1.

[21] Burke, *Old Man River*, 248–9.

[22] Lackmeyer and Money, *OKC*, 110.

variety of downtown improvements; possibilities included new hotels (there was only one downtown), a sports complex able to accommodate NFL, NBA, or NHL teams, retail stores and restaurants, a renovated convention center and music hall, a Native American Cultural Center, a marina, and facilities for water, hiking, biking, and equestrian activities. "This vision will take at least 15, perhaps 20 years," Ackerman said in presenting his proposal, "but when it is complete, our city will be competitive with any city in the nation."[23]

The next stop for the proposal was City Hall. Mayor Norick, who had participated in the Shawnee retreat and was still contemplating what the city might do to avoid future experiences such as the loss of the United Airlines facility, was open to a plan to turn the city around.[24] In January 1992, the mayor created a Metro Area Projects Task Force that included himself, city manager Don Bown, county commissioner F.G. "Buck" Buchanan, county treasurer Joe Barnes, and Chamber of Commerce chairman Frank McPherson. (Ackerman's term as chairman had been completed by this time.) The group's goals, Norick said, were to gather sufficient information to determine which of the brick-and-mortar projects under discussion would best move Oklahoma City in the direction of becoming "a big league city" and then create a plan to fund and build them.[25]

The "Vision" list created by Ackerman and the Chamber of Commerce formed a starting point for the task force's work. The Chamber provided staff support and funding to hire Florida-based facilities consultant Rick Horrow to help evaluate and cost out

---

[23] Ibid.

[24] Oklahoma City, it should be noted, operates with a weak mayor/city manager government structure. The mayor's position is part-time, paying only $24,000 a year in 2011; mayors keep their day jobs, and Norick was operating in many ways as a civic volunteer—hence his treatment as an urban statesman.

[25] Parker, "MAP to the Future: Norick Feeling Easy Down Final Stretch," 12 December 1993, News 1.

stadium, arena, and convention center proposals and Thomas Keilhorn & Associates to conduct a variety of public opinion surveys. The group also brought in architectural and engineering firm Frankfurt Short Bruza (FSB) to help with costing potential proposals.[26] Norick, who wanted to develop a formal proposal before people started dissecting it, hoped to keep initial discussions under the media radar, explaining, "Everybody [on the task force] likes the ideas, but nobody knows if they will work.... I darn sure don't want [the press] finding out about it, because it just would get barbecued. It just isn't ready for prime time viewing yet."[27] His fears proved somewhat unfounded. The *Daily Oklahoman* reported the task force's work anyway, but aside from reporting that the group met in closed session, the treatment of its purported product was friendly.[28]

Ironically, Ackerman's river proposal was not initially on the list. Norick's main goal was to maintain and update the facilities already in existence. Oklahoma City, he realized, had not built or significantly renovated a public facility in twenty years.[29] All around him were facility emergencies: the Triple-A ball team was threatening to leave town because of the state of the ballpark; horseshows were threatening to bail out because of the state of the fairgrounds; the Convention Center was old and unattractive—not an easy sell to the convention crowd.[30] It took Ackerman's continued heavy lobbying for a project he said would beautify and unify the city to insure its inclusion.

On 15 September 1993, a list of nine projects, dubbed MAPS (Metropolitan Area Projects), was officially revealed. The proposals,

---

[26] Lackmeyer and Money, *OKC*, 112–14.

[27] Lackmeyer and Money, *OKC*, 115.

[28] John Parker, "Panel Examining Plans to Put City Among U.S. Best," *Daily Oklahoman*, 30 November 1993, News, 1.

[29] Randy Krehbiel, "Drawing MAPS to Success," *Tulsa World* (Tulsa, OK), 19 July 1999, Focus, 13.

[30] Gypsy Hogan, "Chamber's Talks Produced Hints of MAPS to Be," *Daily Oklahoman*, 1 August 1999, Business, 1.

selected based on both the task force's evaluation and polling numbers,[31] included a 12,000-seat baseball park, to be built to AAA-league standards; a 20,000-seat indoor arena built to NBA/NHL standards; a new downtown library; renovation of the Myriad Convention Center and the Civic Center Music Hall; and renovations to the Oklahoma State Fairgrounds. Connecting them all were a trolley transit system and a redeveloped North Canadian River and a Riverwalk/canal into downtown, Ackerman's dream.[32] Not on the list was one project with significant backing: a new downtown art museum. (The citizens supporting that project were able, through private fund-raising and a Reynolds Foundation challenge grant, to make it happen anyway.) Now there was a vision; how would they bring it to life?

A Plan of Action

Norick, Ackerman, and other backers of MAPS made several strategic decisions that would prove important to the success of the proposal. First, they decided to structure the referendum as an all-or-nothing vote. Most of the projects on the list had previously appeared as stand-alone choices on a referendum ballot. In 1986, for example, library, fair ground, and convention center upgrades tied to sales or hotel/motel tax increases appeared as separate ballot items, along with a variety of other initiatives, as part of a plan dubbed "Six to Fix." Although bond issues related to police, fire, and street improvements passed, all of the big downtown improvement projects failed to win support—each opposed by a separate constituency.[33]

Norick feared that if voters were once again given the opportunity to vote for their individual favorites, voters would pick and choose among the available choices, and few or none would gather sufficient votes to pass. Initial polling indicated that only the river project and

---

[31] Charles Van Rysselberge, interview, 15 December 2011.
[32] Lackmeyer and Money, *OKC*, 115–21.
[33] Lackmeyer and Money, *OKC*, 102.

the new downtown library were likely to be approved if the projects were voted on individually—and the river was a close call. If the projects were voted on separately, Norick warned, "If we are lucky, we are maybe going to pass a couple of things, or, if we are really lucky, three. But then what have [we] got? A hodge-podge—a mess." The city would have once again dreamed big and come up short. To solve the problem all of the projects were placed on a single ballot, to be paid for using a five-year, one-penny sales tax. The tax money would go only for projects on the list until all were complete.[34]

Second, the group felt the failure of the "Six to Fix" plan reflected a lack of confidence by the community in the ability of the city government to complete the projects in an efficient and timely fashion. To deal with the credibility issue, they included in the legislation a citizen oversight committee to ensure that the projects were properly bid on and completed, and emphasized the "pay-as-you-go" nature of the plan.[35]

Finally, they determined not to wait to hold the referendum. Here again, opinion polling was part of the decision. Polls by Thomas Keilhorn & Associates indicated that the community at large was pessimistic about the economic outlook for the area, and that, taken on an individual basis, there was little enthusiasm for large-scale downtown cultural projects. Several on the task force felt that the vote should wait until after the next mayoral election in 1994, so that Norick would not be endangering his chance of reelection if the vote failed. Norick, however, wanted to push ahead. "I don't want to be mayor if we don't at least try to do this," he told the group. "If we take a shot at this, and it doesn't pass and that results in me not being reelected, then so be it."[36] Norick prevailed. In October 1993, the city council decided to call a special election for 14 December 1993.[37]

---

[34] Lackmeyer and Money, *OKC*, 121.
[35] Lackmeyer and Money, *OKC*, 116, 122.
[36] Lackmeyer and Money, *OKC*, 114.
[37] Lackmeyer and Money, *OKC*, 124.

Going into the election, prospects for passage of the measure did not look bright. Opinion polling early in the campaign showed that while 53 percent of voters favored the proposed renovation of the convention center, only 41 percent favored a new ball park, 48 percent favored the river improvements, and 44 percent a new sports arena. Sixty-four percent of respondents said they thought city sales taxes were high enough. "While a slim majority thought the city should do something to revive downtown," Lackmeyer and Money reported, "an equal number believed that taxes should only be spent for public safety, street improvements, and other vital services instead of projects like those proposed in MAPS." Anticipating a legal challenge, Norick requested an opinion from the city attorney indicating that it was legal to use sales tax money—as opposed to a bond issue—to fund such projects.[38]

By election day, thanks to a "Believe in Our Future" campaign largely financed and run by the Chamber of Commerce and hard campaigning by Norick, pollsters indicated that the tide had turned. Norick told the *Daily Oklahoman*, "I'm very optimistic that the voters will approve the plan, but I think it's going to be a pretty close election."[39] Even though "early tabulations were tense for both sides, as only a few hundred votes separated the issue until about 9 p.m.," MAPS was approved by a 54-percent majority on 14 December 1993. "Oklahoma City, welcome to the big leagues," Norick celebrated. "You wait until those phones start ringing tomorrow morning wanting to know what's happening in Oklahoma City. This community in the year 2000 is going to be so strong and so vibrant."[40]

---

[38] Ibid.

[39] Lackmeyer and Money, *OKC*, 129.

[40] John Parker, "Voters OK Tax, Downtown Projects," *Daily Oklahoman*, 15 December 1994, News, 1.

The Build-out

It would take every bit of that time and more to realize the dream. Eager as they were to have construction begin, voters had only a series of watercolor sketches and campaign promises—not shovel-ready plans.[41] Even though Norick initially spoke of breaking ground on the baseball park, the first dam on the river project, and the library in 1994, acquiring land, preparing architectural and engineering studies, and letting bids took time. Most of 1994 was spent constructing a MAPS master plan. Even though the bombing of the Alfred P. Murrah Federal Building on 19 April 1995 diverted the community's attention and energy, citizens anxiously waited for construction on some part of the project to begin. Sports columnist John Rohde, frustrated by the politicking and slow pace associated with MAPS, expressed the sentiments of the community at large: "Obviously, we all want MAPS to be handled correctly. But let's pick up the pace. How 'bout it, MAPS people? Sign some contracts. Dig a hole. Move some dirt. Lay some concrete. Plow down the old. Start building the new. When can you start? Sometime yesterday would be nice."[42]

Groundbreaking for the ballpark, a strictly ceremonial event, occurred on 11 October 1995. Following a long string of complications and delays, a contract was finally awarded in July 1996, and construction began in September. While there were other problems, the most serious of which was a revenue shortfall that threatened to shelve the arena project, the beginning of the ballpark construction broke a logjam, and other construction soon began.[43] The first project completed was the ballpark, which opened for business on 17 April

---

[41] Lackmeyer and Money, *OKC*, 144–45.

[42] John Rohde, "MAPS Must Pick Up the Pace," *Daily Oklahoman*, 9 March 1995, Sports, 21.

[43] For details, see Lackmeyer and Money, *OKC*, 149–53.

1998, with Norick throwing out the first pitch in front of a sell-out crowd.[44]

Throwing that pitch was Norick's last task before leaving the public arena. In November 1997, the mayor had announced that he would not seek a fourth term. A seven-man race developed, with the central issue being if and how the MAPS effort would be completed. While most of the candidates argued for shelving plans to construct a new arena, Kirk Humphries, the eventual winner, campaigned on the slogan "Finish MAPS Right," arguing that the solution to the revenue shortfall was to extend the sales tax for six months in order that all the projects could be completed. Norick favored this approach, and had attempted to get city council approval for placing a tax extension on the ballot in 1997.[45] Humphries came close to winning the election outright, and trounced his run-off opponent by carrying 70 percent of the vote. (The race was hard-fought, however. The final two candidates spent $500,000 between them for a job that paid just $2,000 a year in 1998.)[46] In a special election in December 1998, a six-month extension of the tax was approved by a two-to-one margin.[47]

Work also proceeded on Ackerman's favorite projects. Construction of the mile-long Bricktown Canal began in July 1998. Initially plagued with design issues and zoning hassles regarding properties fronting the canal, the finished product, which featured two waterfalls, several sidewalk plazas, parks, and an interactive fountain, opened on 2 July 1999 with 40,000 people in attendance.[48] The canal so excited the citizenry that many could not wait for the opening. Thousands flocked to the area and broke through the construction fencing to get an early view; two subcontractors even cruised the canal in a ski boat, escaping before police could catch

---

[44] Lackmeyer and Money, *OKC*, 156.

[45] Lackmeyer and Money, *OKC*, 152–53.

[46] Lackmeyer and Money, *OKC*, 156.

[47] Lackmeyer and Money, *OKC*, 171.

[48] "'This is Just Great:' Canal Opens; 40,000 Hit Bricktown," *Daily Oklahoman*, 3 July 1999, News, 1.

them.[49] Opening day featured water taxi rides, food and drink, speeches by dignitaries—and the first "official" illegal swimmer, pulled from the water by police at 9 p.m.[50]

Construction on the river dams began in the summer 1999. Assisted by funding from the Army Corps of Engineers, the $52 million project officially opened 11 December 2004, the last of the nine MAPS projects to be completed.[51] In May 2004, the seven-mile stretch of water was officially renamed the Oklahoma River, following another campaign by Ackerman directed at the state legislature.[52] His final river effort targeted his alma mater, Oklahoma City University: he contacted the vice president of development and suggested that OCU make rowing a varsity sport, to take advantage of the venue. It happened; the river now boasts a string of university boathouses and an Olympic-quality rowing facility and hosts several major competitions.

Although they were clearly not the only people involved in the conception and implementation of the original MAPS initiative, Ackerman and Norick are the names most frequently associated with its success in the Oklahoma City community. Ackerman is credited with the initial vision; Norick gets credit for making it happen.

Ackerman's particular genius lay in his ability to envision paradise in a place where others saw only a dustbowl. He was especially frustrated with those who refused the see the North Canadian as a "real" river. "[I]t is a river," he insisted. "We just need to put a couple of dams in it. Hell, half the lakes in the world started because they dammed up rivers."[53] He was convinced the river was

---

[49] Lackmeyer and Money, *OKC*, 174.

[50] "Canal Facts," *Daily Oklahoman*, 3 July 1999, News, 10.

[51] Jake Trotter and Jesse Olivarez, "MAPS: Holiday parade and festival officially open crosstown waterway—crowd celebrates river's fresh start," *Daily Oklahoman*, 12 December 2004, News, 16A.

[52] Carmet Perez Snyder, "River's new name a dream come true," *Daily Oklahoman*, 22 May 2004, News, 1A.

[53] Lackmeyer and Money, *OKC*, 111.

central to Oklahoma City's image, good or bad. In a speech to the downtown Kiwanis Club in February 1991, he argued, "[W]hen companies, interested in us as a possible relocation site or for a new plant, come to see us, they travel over the river from the airport and see people cutting weeds on one side and toasting marshmallows on the other right there in the river bed and that, ladies and gentlemen, creates a dry and dusty image."[54] The cure for Oklahoma City's problems, he thought, had to be an idea capable of transforming the city, and of changing the mindset of the people who lived there.

Norick's contribution lay in his ability to get things done; he was more a builder than a dreamer. He was able to take the visionary project list created by Ackerman and the Chamber board, break it into achievable parts, figure out how to finance it, and get the construction started. In doing so, he created a model that would serve his community on repeated occasions.

The success of MAPS is, in many ways, assessable from its aftermath. In 2001, a second set of MAPS projects went before the voters. Dubbed "MAPS for Kids," the initiative combined a designated sales tax with a school bond issue to fund more than one hundred Oklahoma City-area school projects, ranging from new school construction to renovation of existing facilities, across a number of school districts. That tax expired in 2008. In 2009, the city passed MAPS 3, a seven-year-nine-month extension of a one-cent sales tax, to fund a new downtown park, a rail-based streetcar system (MAPS 1 stopped with trolleys), street improvements, biking and walking trails, aquatic centers throughout the city, improvements to the Oklahoma River and the state fair grounds, and a new convention center. (The expanded Convention Center built with MAPS 1 funds was so successful the city had already outgrown it. Since 1993, the number of conventions had increased significantly, and the number of downtown hotels available to support the convention trade had increased from one to ten.) The initiative passed with 54 percent of

---

[54] Sidebar in Lackmeyer and Money, *OKC*, 111.

the vote. In pushing for the original MAPS projects, boosters argued that the initiative would generate $140 million in private investment and bring Oklahoma City into the big leagues. Within ten years, Lackmeyer and Money reported, more than a billion dollars of public and private investment had occurred. [55]

Perhaps more importantly, the MAPS story and the work of Ackerman and Norick provided a model for other urban statesmen. This kind of initiative is transferable. Charles Van Rysselberge, who served as the president of the Greater Oklahoma City Chamber of Commerce during much of the MAPS 1 era, makes the point: "After Oklahoma City, I served as CEO of the Charleston [South Carolina] Chamber for nine years. Charleston has so many assets—blocks and blocks of historic buildings, a mayor who has been in office for 35 years, a beautiful setting, and lots of history. It was significant in the Revolutionary and Civil Wars. But none of that can be replicated. Oklahoma City can be replicated anywhere."[56]

Elements of Oklahoma City's project will reappear as we examine the work of other urban statesmen. Salt Lake City business executives used their tax structure to fund transportation projects, and Columbus, Georgia, statesman John Turner, like Ackerman, was inspired by a river. But before considering those stories, I want to discuss an example of urban statesmanship in action with which I was personally involved. Let's head to Atlanta, where another combination of business leaders with complementary talents saved a large public hospital from financial disaster.

---

[55] Lackmeyer and Money, *OKC*, 185.
[56] Charles Van Rysselberge interview, 15 December 2011.

4

Atlanta: Saving Grady[1]

On a crisp evening in late 2006, Pete Correll and Tom Bell, two of Atlanta's most admired business leaders, sat nursing cocktails in a restaurant on the ground floor of the 191 Peachtree Tower where both men had their offices.

They were friends, and laughter came easily. But that night both men looked drawn and serious.

Correll, the retired chairman of paper giant Georgia-Pacific, and his wife of forty-three years, Ada Lee, were chairing the capital campaign for Emory Medical School. Their interest was personal as well as philanthropic; both Corrells credited Emory University Hospital with providing them outstanding medical care that saved their lives.[2] As part of their "homework" in their quest to raise $500 million for the school, they had spent the day visiting all the emergency rooms where Emory doctors practiced. One of them was

---

[1] Much of the information in this case study comes from interviews with Pete Correll, Tom Bell, and Michael Russell, our three urban statesmen. I was also a key participant in the events I'm detailing here, as were Metro Atlanta Chamber staffers Esther Campi, Renay Blumenthal, and Che Watkins. Rather than footnote their every word, I will simply let the story flow and note other sources when I use them.

[2] According to an Emory University Woodruff Health Sciences Center press release issued 23 March 2007, "…more than a decade ago…Ada Lee Correll had a cardiogram as part of her annual physical at Emory which resulted in open heart surgery the next day. Five years later, doctors in Emory University Hospital's Emergency Department revived Pete Correll after a major heart attack. More recently, Emory doctors detected an early-stage cancer and removed one kidney." The press release can be found at http://whsc.emory.edu/presss_releases_print.cfm?announcement_id_seq=9460.

Grady Memorial Hospital, the site of Atlanta's only Level 1 trauma center and the place where one in four Georgia doctors was trained. It was also Atlanta's "safety-net" hospital, and, like many urban hospitals, it teetered on the brink of financial collapse in the wake of skyrocketing healthcare costs and dwindling revenues from patients who couldn't pay.

Correll knew all this before he visited Grady's emergency room. Still, what he saw there shocked him, especially in contrast to the sparkling, high-tech facilities at Emory's campus hospital and another in Midtown.

"I saw the damndest thing today," Correll told Bell, who ran the prominent Atlanta real-estate investment trust Cousins Properties. "I went to Emory and saw world-class technology and world-class resources. And I went over to Grady and it was like going into a third-world country."

In his decades as a businessman and philanthropist, Correll had seen a lot. He had served on a long list of corporate and non-profit boards and raised money for most of the big charities in town. But this time he was shaken. Patients on gurneys lined the hall. Doctors and nurses were forced to track patients and procedures on outdated chalkboards. Premature babies were being kept alive in jerry-rigged incubators.

A serious Bell just nodded: "Pete, it's worse than you think."

Bell was in a position to know. As a board member for Emory Healthcare and chairman of its audit committee, he had seen the numbers. Grady, a $700 million business with five thousand employees serving more than a million patients every year, was running out of cash. In fact, it was imploding. The medical staff serving Grady comprised professors, doctors, and medical students from Emory and Morehouse medical schools under contract to Grady. The hospital was more than a year behind in reimbursing the medical schools for these services—not a sustainable business model.

"In six months," Bell declared, "they'll close their doors if *somebody* doesn't do something,"

A few drinks later, they were convinced: That "somebody" was them.

Grady was still on Correll's mind the next morning, and he phoned Bell to continue their conversation. "How the hell are we going to do this?" he asked. "I'm an unemployed CEO and you're in a real-estate company in the worst damn real-estate recession in history. We've got to have a forum, because right now nobody thinks there's a problem." Grady's long history of "crying wolf" when the financial going got tough would work against them, he felt, if they tried to push the issue forward on their own.

Their next call was to me. Both men had served as chairman of the Metro Atlanta Chamber and had led Chamber task forces addressing public policy issues. Both were serving on the Chamber's Executive Committee.

"We want the Chamber to tackle Grady Hospital," they said. "The community needs to do this, and there's no better place, no better forum, and quite frankly there's no better ally than the Chamber." The Chamber had a long history of addressing controversial issues, including regional water and transportation issues, the redesign of the Georgia state flag, and support for Atlanta's Olympic bid, in a calm and evenhanded manner. Both Bell and Correll felt that the Chamber's fact-driven approach to issues, with which they were acquainted from previous Chamber projects, would temper the emotion and the political drama that any attempt to change Grady would generate.

I wasn't so sure. First, the perception that Grady Hospital was on the verge of financial collapse had been around for years, but nobody really knew the facts of the situation. Was the hospital really about to fall apart, or were they just looking for a quick infusion of funds so they could postpone addressing their problems for another few years? Second, I wondered if this was really a place where the business community could make a unique difference. It seemed to me that there might be other parties who should address Grady's issues, particularly since the hospital was governed by a public authority— the Fulton-DeKalb Hospital Authority (FDHA)—that belonged to Fulton and DeKalb counties. Third, the FDHA had not asked for our help. I was concerned that we would be seen as outsiders poking our noses into an area in which we were unwelcome. Finally, although the Chamber had a strong history of dealing with biracial issues, a focus on Grady, regarded in the city as an African-American institution, had the potential for creating tremendous racial and political tension. I needed to be sure that the Chamber's board was prepared for the accusation that they were meddling where they did not belong, and that they would stand behind the effort if our involvement provoked a confrontation.

The Grady Story

A bit of background might be helpful here. Founded in 1892, Grady Hospital was initially owned and operated by the City of Atlanta, with a private self-perpetuating board of trustees. In 1941, following the passage of the Georgia Hospital Authorities Act, the hospital's governance was shifted to the Fulton-DeKalb Hospital Authority, a ten-person board whose members were appointed by the county commissions of Fulton and DeKalb counties—seven from Fulton, three from DeKalb.[3] The Fulton representatives were appointed by, and thus beholden to, individual county commissioners; the DeKalb authority members were appointed by the county CEO and confirmed by the commission. Inherent in this structure was the exposure of authority members to political pressure.

---

[3] The Metro Atlanta Chamber houses a private collection of papers related to the Greater Grady Task Force. They will be henceforth cited as "MAC, Grady Papers." This information comes from the Greater Grady Final Task Force Report in MAC, Grady Papers (13 July 2007 meeting notebook) 16.

The two counties funded the indigent healthcare provided to their populations by Grady, although their contributions to Grady's budget had remained essentially flat since the late 1990s and funded only about 60 percent of their indigent healthcare costs in 2007.[4] The hospital did not receive direct contributions from other counties whose patients used the hospital, especially its trauma unit or burn center, or from the state, although it did receive some federal funding.

In 2007 (and this is also true today), Grady saw more than 30,000 inpatients and about one million outpatients a year.[5] Only about 8 percent of the hospital's patients had private insurance. Uninsured and Medicaid patients made up about 75 percent of the total patient load. Slightly less than 60 percent of the hospital's revenue came from Medicaid and Medicare, which reimbursed approximately 80 percent of the cost of caring for each patient.[6] The result was that Grady consistently ran a deficit. In fact, the hospital was expected to end 2007 $53 million in the red[7] and held a $71 million debt to the Emory and Morehouse schools of medicine for doctor salaries.[8] So if what Pete Correll and Tom Bell were telling me and the board of the Metro Atlanta Chamber was true—if Grady's closure was imminent—then the hospital's closure would result in many of Atlanta's hospital emergency rooms, both urban and suburban, being flooded with patients who would not be able to pay for the services they received.

---

[4] Pam Stephenson, Grady 101 presentation to Task Force, in MAC, Grady Papers (11 April 2007 meeting notebook).

[5] Greater Grady Task Force Final Report, in MAC, Grady Papers (13 July 2007 meeting notebook) 15.

[6] Stephenson, Grady 101 presentation, 11 April 2007.

[7] Alvarez & Marsal, "Grady Health System Plan of Operations (executive summary)," in MAC, Grady Papers (Spring 2007, notebook 1) 11.

[8] Shaila Dewan and Kevin Sack, "A Safety-Net Hospital Falls into Financial Crisis," *New York Times*, 8 January 2008, http://www.nytimes.com/2008/01/08/us/08grady.html?pagewanted=print, accessed 5 November 2012.

Correll called the potential consequences a "patient tsunami" that would cause a near collapse of emergency care in the metropolitan region.

I explained my hesitance to Correll and Bell, who disagreed but, being familiar with the Chamber's process, chose to respect my position. In effect, they cut a deal with me. They left me and the rest of the board to gather information and further educate ourselves about the situation, and they tackled the task of convincing Fulton and DeKalb counties and the FDHA to ask for and accept our assistance with solving Grady's financial problems.

Bell, working with Atlanta City Council President Lisa Borders, arranged a meeting with State Representative Pam Stephenson and Dr. Chris Edwards, the chair and vice-chair of the Fulton-DeKalb Hospital Authority. Correll and I met with Vernon Jones, CEO of DeKalb County, and Fulton County Commission Chairman John Eaves. Correll and Bell also approached Atlanta Mayor Shirley Franklin who, although concerned about the state of the hospital and its continued viability, felt it inappropriate to get involved with an authority that belonged to another governmental entity.

Correll and Bell's message was simple: "We know you know the hospital is in trouble. The Metro Atlanta Chamber has a lot of experience with large businesses and we think we can provide you with some helpful insights. If you'd like us to help, ask us to do so and we will."

On 28 February 2007, after several conversations between Chamber officials, Correll, Bell, and FDHA board officials Stephenson and Edwards, Tom Bell received a letter from FDHA chair Stephenson inviting the Chamber to participate in an evaluation of Grady's issues. The Chamber board, chaired by AT&T's Richard A. Anderson, responded on March 15 by authorizing the appointment of a task force, to be chaired by Correll and H.J. Russell & Company CEO Michael Russell, son of Herman Russell, who founded one of the largest African-American construction companies in the US. The seventeen-person racially balanced task force, including representatives of business, government, health care institutions, and civic organizations and assisted by Deloitte Consulting on a *pro bono* basis, was formally appointed April 2, setting a ninety-day timeline.[9]

The Metro Atlanta Chamber assigned three full-time professional staff members to the task force to manage consultants, conduct research, maintain a liaison with elected officials, prepare briefing materials for the task force, and communicate with the media and stakeholders. Senior Vice President for Public Policy Renay Blumenthal, Senior Vice President for Communications and Marketing Esther Campi, and Vice President for Government Affairs Che Watkins spent countless hours anticipating information needs and responding to requests from Correll, Bell, and Russell.

Toes in the Water

The Greater Grady Task Force was dipping its toes into a fast-flowing stream. One of our first tasks was to determine the nature and extent of Grady's financial problem. And as Bell noted, "We needed to convince folks we needed to save Grady. They needed to know it was their problem, that we needed the hospital in terms of trauma care and also in terms of the number of patients Grady covered that would load up every hospital in the area if Grady were not there." If people did not believe that the Grady situation was at a tipping point, particularly the people on the FDHA board and the Fulton and DeKalb county commissions, the chances any study would actually result in change were slim.

Persuading the Atlanta community at large of the need to maintain Grady turned out to be one of our easier tasks. Correll and Bell made the rounds to Rotary Clubs and other business and civic organizations, describing the impact of a closed Grady on medical care in the urban and suburban Atlanta area. The specter of inaccessible emergency rooms proved to be a compelling image. Our

---

[9] Grady timeline, in MAC, Grady Papers (notebook 2).

fear that the more affluent areas of the city would see Grady's crisis as "not my problem" did not materialize; we found that these sectors of the community generally supported our efforts.

The FDHA board was already working with consultants Alvarez & Marsal (A&M), who were completing an extensive review of both Grady's financial situation and its operational structure. The firm (which the FDHA fired in May before its report was formalized) had identified a number of problems with both Grady's operations and its governing structure and recommended extensive changes to both. One thing the A&M report made clear was that while simply streamlining the hospital's operations would save millions of dollars, the savings would not be enough to avert the looming financial crisis.

Another popular perception was that if Grady were paid for its uninsured patients who came from counties other than Fulton and DeKalb, there would be no financial crisis. Renay Blumenthal persuaded Georgia State University's Health Policy Center to conduct a study which showed that while, in fact, Grady treated indigent patients from outside Fulton and DeKalb counties, those other counties also received Fulton and DeKalb patients—a pattern of cross-boundary care that held throughout the state. "Truing up" the uninsured patient-care costs, while something that should probably be done, was not going to generate sufficient funds to make a dent in Grady's problems.[10] Data provided by the Georgia Hospital Association suggested that such a process would generate only about $3.1 million for the sample year of 2006—not an insignificant amount but nowhere near enough to close the $50 million annual operating deficit Grady was facing at the time.[11]

---

[10] Georgia Health Policy Center, "Grady's Market and the Uninsured," prepared for the Greater Grady Task Force, in MAC, Grady Papers (25 June 2007 meeting notebook).

[11] Georgia Hospital Association, "County Data," in MAC, Grady Papers (13 July 2007 meeting notebook). See also Metro Atlanta Chamber, Greater Grady Task Force Final Report, in MAC, Grady Papers (13 July 2007 meeting notesbook) 4.

Additionally, the Greater Grady Task Force reported that every major urban hospital authority in the state had converted its governing entity to a nonprofit 501(c)(3) model, giving the hospitals the ability to raise funds from sources other than government, develop a range of profitable services to help underwrite indigent care, and place themselves on a more equal footing with competitors.[12]

Grady's overall funding needs totaled $370 million ($120 million in short-term funding to overhaul operations, pay the medical schools for doctors' salaries, and address immediate capital needs identified by A&M, and $250 million for badly needed, long-term capital improvements), plus $50 million every year to cover an annual operating deficit. Clearly, new sources of funds were needed and, the task force argued after three months of study, those sources would not be available unless the governing structure of the hospital was changed. History suggested that the county and state governments were not likely to increase their contributions to the hospital, and no foundation was likely to give money to a hospital with such an intensely political governing entity.[13]

Restructuring the governance of the hospital, allowing the current authority to remain the owner and establishing a contractual arrangement with a new 501(c)(3) nonprofit organization for operating the hospital, was the chief recommendation of the final Greater Grady Task Force report, delivered on 13 July 2007. The report concluded:

> While Grady's challenges are daunting, the hospital can and must be saved. The critical first step is the restructure, and the first "domino" that has to happen is the Grady board's willingness and leadership to take this bold step. This task force and the leadership of the business community/Metro Atlanta Chamber stand ready to assist if asked.

---

[12] Ibid., 16.

[13] Metro Atlanta Chamber, Greater Grady Task Force Final Report, "Key Grady Takeaways," in MAC, Grady Papers (13 July 2007 meeting notebook) 4.

> The task force is also prepared to recommend a highly effective slate of community leaders of the caliber and expertise needed to serve on the new 501(c)(3) board.[14]

The Atlanta Way

Running as an undercurrent throughout the task force process was the issue of race. Michael Russell, co-chair of the task force, is also the CEO of Atlanta's premier black-owned construction business. He heard it all; the rumors circulating included: that the business community was making a real-estate play trying to get access to Grady's land, that the white business community really wanted to close Grady, that Emory Medical School was trying to make a profit off the backs of Atlanta's poor.

A group known as the Grady Coalition appeared regularly at Grady board meetings and the Chamber office, protesting the work of the task force before the recommendations even appeared. Coalition member Ron Marshall accused the business community of seeking to gain control over "the millions in contracts in the hospital system's $730 million budget."[15] State Senator Vincent Fort repeatedly expressed his concern that a new nonprofit board would slash services to the poor to improve the hospital's bottom line, and accused the board and the task force of "a pattern of secrecy" and "a strong-arm job." [16] Once our report was published, Joe Beasley, Southern Regional Director of the Rainbow/PUSH Coalition, criticized the final proposal as a "power grab by the white business community,[17] and the Rev. Tim McDonald, who was involved with

---

[14] Ibid., 5.

[15] Craig Schneider, "Vote set for today: Critical test for Grady's board," *Atlanta Journal-Constitution*, 26 November 2007, A1.

[16] Craig Schneider and Gayle White, "Grady split seems to heal," *Atlanta Journal-Constitution*, 28 December 2007, A1; and "Grady's National accreditation at risk," *Atlanta Journal-Constitution*, 4 December 2007, A1.

[17] Gayle White, "Grady board nominee was task force member," *Atlanta Journal-Constitution*, 15 August 2007, B4.

both the Grady Coalition and another prominent organization, Concerned Black Clergy, argued that "white leaders are using the specter of Grady closing as a 'scare tactic' to get support for their plan."[18]

The tension was such that Correll, at the meeting where the final task force report was presented, felt compelled to say, "The work of the Task Force and the recommendations that we have made should not be construed as a 'white takeover' of a 'black board.' At the end of the day, this is not a black or white issue, but a green one—green meaning money. And I believe that everyone involved in this process has only been focused on what is best for Grady and how we can raise this money to save one of the most venerable institutions in our state."

The biracial composition of the task force, and Russell's presence in particular, did much to dull the impact of those arguments. "My being the co-chair of the task force and being African American and being from Atlanta, people knew I didn't have an agenda of any sort and would bring some credibility to the fact that this was really an effort to make sure Grady Hospital survived," Russell says. The fact that he was a "Grady baby," as those born at the hospital were known, did not hurt either. He, along with City Council President Lisa Borders, organized a meeting with an important community organization, the Concerned Black Clergy, which was key to the success of the task force's work.

The meeting, a quarterly prayer breakfast hosted by Borders, took place on 18 September 2007 at the Georgia Freight Depot. Russell asked Chamber staff member Che Watkins, a prominent African-American graduate of Spelman College, to summarize the group's recommendations, including a discussion of the myths and rumors swirling around the report. Watkins recalls a long question-and-answer session following her presentation, which ended with a

---

[18] Gayle White, "A Question of Black and White," *Atlanta Journal-Constitution*, 10 August 2007, A1.

question from the Rev. Joseph Lowery: "He asked me, 'Is this all you want to do?' I said, 'Yes sir, this is it in a nutshell.' He said, 'All right, I can work with that.'" [19]

Russell then talked to the clergy about the study and its recommendations and authenticated the facts. He said, "This is not a racial take-over. This thing's going down so we need to push the racial innuendos aside and take a hard look at whether we want the biggest charity hospital in the city to go down—and by the way, its major constituents are members of your churches." In retrospect, it is clear that this meeting was critical to allowing the implementation of the changes we were proposing as it allowed the black clergy and those they influenced to say, "We've heard from Joe Beasley, from Vincent Fort, from Emma Darnell, from Bill Edwards (all African-American politicians who were opposed to our involvement), but we have to have our hospital fixed."

As a result, says Russell, "[The critics] were a vocal minority. But if you really pulled back the covers and you talked to the black people in the community, there was generally an acceptance for, 'What can we do to save Grady?'" A later meeting with the Concerned Black Clergy at Providence Missionary Baptist Church, where Pete Correll joined Russell, allowed us to reinforce our position. But it took Michael Russell and Lisa Borders with their impeccable credentials in the black community to say, "Here it is." Pete or Tom or I could not have done that.

One way we chose to deal with the accusation that the white business community was out to take over a major black institution was to be as open and transparent as possible in all of our actions. Early in the process, demonstrators were gathering at every major Chamber event and Grady Board meeting, Protests outside the Chamber offices became so common that we even began serving coffee and doughnuts. Pete Correll committed to Esther Campi—then the Chamber's Senior Vice President for Communications and

---

[19] Che Watkins interview, 10 September 2012.

Marketing—to do whatever it took to get the task force's story out. He insisted that all meetings be open to the public. Correll and Campi placed themselves aggressively in front of the press, calling and briefing reporters both on the record and on background, setting up press conferences—taking questions, says Esther, "until the last dog died"—so the media knew we had nothing to hide. The press attended every task-force meeting, and task-force leadership was available to answer questions on each of those occasions.

Campi describes Correll as a "disarmingly candid" spokesman. Accused of orchestrating a white takeover of a black institution, he'd assure his detractors that he was not a racist, that the board and the management team of the hospital would reflect the diversity of the community—and that the fact he was white was just one of those unavoidable annoyances. He agreed to guarantee that Grady would always serve as a safety-net hospital caring for the underprivileged. Particularly telling was the evolution of his relationship with one of our most vocal opponents, the Rev. Tim McDonald of the Grady Coalition and Concerned Black Clergy. As the task force developed its recommendations and then proceeded to implement them, McDonald and Correll often exchanged words. But they also got to know one another, and that made a difference. "First and foremost, I'm a pastor," McDonald says. "Pete Correll's cancer came back, and I talked with him about that. I saw a side of him that I had not seen in a board meeting. We talked about Brunswick [Georgia], where both of us are from. We talked about how Brunswick has changed over the years, and we talked about how Grady was going to change and how Grady needed to change. And I began to see him in a different light, and I began to communicate that with my other Coalition partners. And I remember saying in one meeting, 'I trust Pete Correll.'"[20]

---

[20] Grady Health Foundation, "The Grady Miracle," (video), http://www.gradyhealthfoundation.org, accessed 25 March 2013.

Beyond the Recommendations

Once the recommendations were presented, a typical Chamber task force would have turned the results of its study over to the people who had requested it for implementation. That was not the way this group chose to operate. As Tom Bell says, "Most task forces define a problem and suggest an approach and then someone else comes in and does it. Here, there was no one else to do the implementation, and if there was no implementation, we would have had failure—a messed-up medical system."

The task force had been clear from the beginning that it had no authority to act and did not intend to get involved in political processes. As the final report was issued, however, the group's leadership—Tom Bell, Pete Correll, and Michael Russell—came to the conclusion that while the existing FDHA board realized that they needed access to increased funding, they were satisfied with the structure at hand, almost to the point of saying to us, "Thank you very much. We appreciate your report. We'll call you when we need you." No changes meant no access to the funding Grady needed to survive, and a financially defunct Grady meant a real mess for the medical community of Atlanta. We simply were not willing to watch while nothing happened, knowing that we knew the solution to the problem.

The FDHA responded to the task force report by hiring the Troutman Sanders law firm to review legal questions surrounding the proposed restructuring and creating what was essentially a task force of their own to review options for the hospital. Over the next couple of months, a number of civic, community and governmental entities offered support for our task force recommendations, among them the Southern Christian Leadership Conference, the Fulton County Commission, and a number of state legislators. DeKalb County CEO Vernon Jones was a major holdout.

Crucial Cocktails

Once again Pete Correll made use of the after-work cocktail to solve a problem. This time his companion was Jimmy Williams, retired chairman of SunTrust bank and chairman of the Woodruff Foundation, Atlanta's premier philanthropic foundation established by long-time Coca-Cola chairman and CEO Robert Woodruff. "The key, of course," says Correll, "was could we raise any money, because to that point we had an idea of what we wanted for a change and none of the political leaders wanted that change."

Correll went to Jimmy Williams and asked, "Will the Woodruff Foundation support us, and would you give [Grady] a gift and then go with me to the other big foundations and tell them that you think it's doable and that you think we've got a chance?"

Williams laid out a lot of conditions—the board structure would have to change, the new board would need to lease the facility from the FDHA as well as manage the hospital, we'd need to get a forty-year lease, we'd have to get the politics out of the process, and the hospital would need a new management team—and when Correll said we'd do those things, Williams responded, "Why don't we give you the whole $200 million?"

Correll didn't give him a chance to change his mind. "That would be a hell of a lot simpler and a hell of a lot quicker," he answered.

"Well," said Williams, "If you do those things I'll go to our board and I think they'll support you." And they did.

That $200 million commitment—whose donor remained anonymous until changes the Woodruff Foundation had requested were formalized—was the final breakthrough. It was the incentive that led the FDHA to let go, because when the Fulton and DeKalb county governments saw $200 million that they wouldn't have to get from their taxpayers, their attitude was: "This hospital is in crisis. It needs money badly; we all agree with that. Neither of our governments wants to put the money in it, but here's somebody who will, and they are asking for concessions, so let's get really serious."

At that point the Fulton and DeKalb commissions intervened with the FDHA and broke the stalemate. I'm not sure we'd have gotten it done if it had not been for Pete Correll's relationship with Jimmy Williams. At the least, I think it would have been a whole different solution than it is today.

Death by a Thousand Meetings

By November, the hospital authority had agreed in principle to implement our major recommendation; they would allow a private, non-profit board to lease and operate the hospital while retaining ownership of the bricks and mortar. For the next four months, we endured "death by a thousand meetings" as we worked out the details of the lease between the hospital authority and the new 501(c)(3) operating board. Pressures from a number of different directions influenced these discussions, which were guided largely by lawyers and were aimed at generating the bylaws governing the relationship between the new board (called Grady Memorial Hospital Corporation or GMHC) and the FDHA. At issue were such questions as: Who would decide what services to continue/discontinue? How would initial GMHC board members be chosen? Who would be responsible for hiring/firing of top hospital management? Issues would appear settled and then resurface when someone on the FDHA board balked. Complicating our discussions were the fact that the then-anonymous donor of the $200 million in capital improvement funds had set certain conditions on its gift, and the legal requirement that the Fulton and DeKalb county commissions approve the final agreements.

To add to the drama, in late January, the day after the FDHA board voted to approve the lease agreement, the same board fired Grady CEO Otis Story and appointed Pam Stephenson, the FDHA board chair who was also a member of the Georgia House of

Representatives, interim CEO at an annual salary of $600,000.[21] Stephenson later indicated her interest in the permanent CEO position; it fell to Pete Correll to inform her that the position would be filled by a nationwide search, and, later, to tell her that the job had gone to someone else.

By the end of February 2008, both the Fulton and DeKalb county commissions had consented to the lease agreement; the final version was ratified by the FDHA on March 1. The new Grady Memorial Hospital Corporation board of directors, named by the FDHA on March 14, included Pete Correll, Tom Bell, and Michael Russell, and on March 17, Pete Correll was elected chairman of the new entity. Even at this point in the process, we were still collecting protesters outside the Chamber; a demonstration on March 12 protested the potential composition of the as-yet unnamed GMHC board and the possibility that Pete Correll might be named as chairman. [22] After some additional scrambling regarding formal approval of the new corporation's tax-exempt status, the lease agreement formally commenced on 20 May 2008.

As I look back over the eighteen months we spent on the Grady restructuring, it's clear to me that the work of our three "urban statesmen"—Michael Russell, Tom Bell, and Pete Correll—was critical to the success of the restructuring effort. They did, indeed, save Grady Hospital, and each contributed to the effort in unique and important ways.

---

[21] There was considerable media outrage over the appointment and the associated salary, particularly when the details of the contract became public in July 2008. See, for instance, Mike King, "Our Opinion: A Very Costly Interim," *Atlanta Journal-Constitution*, 10 July 2008, A10.

[22] Craig Schneider, "Activists protest Grady board; Group expresses concern for poor," *Atlanta Journal-Constitution*, 12 March 2008, B1; email from Sam Williams to Pete Correll, 11 March 2008, contained in MAC Grady Papers (notebook 2).

The Ambassador

Michael Russell was our ambassador to the African-American community. His biggest single contribution was the meeting he and Lisa Borders hosted with the Concerned Black Clergy.

From the beginning of the task force State Representative Vincent Fort, the Rev. Joe Beasley, and the Rev. Tim McDonald of the Grady Coalition were carrying on a constant fight against us in the press and in public, protesting at the Chamber and at Grady board meetings. But the mainstream black community had not yet taken a position on our proposal. Mayor Shirley Franklin was committed to keeping the hospital open, but did not want the solution to its problems to become a racial issue. She was also concerned about impinging on someone else's political space.

Russell and Borders convinced the Concerned Black Clergy that Grady, the provider of much of the medical care for their parishioners, really would close, that the task force proposal was the best solution to Grady's problems, and that they should take a stand. It worked. Their support, the biracial composition of the task force, and Russell's and Borders's credibility in the black community all contributed to our success, and all exemplified Atlanta's biracial approach to problem solving.

This was, however, far from Russell's only contribution to the exercise. Both Pete Correll and Tom Bell were very much "get it done; do it yesterday, preferably in the morning" types, and there were times when we just could not bulldoze our way through things. Russell's style was more judicious, and he had a balancing effect on their sense of immediacy that was very valuable, particularly when it came to dealing with the political structure.

Also invaluable—and Michael knew this—was the diversity he provided at the leadership level. We had to have African-American participation at the top. "By being involved at the beginning, by staying involved, and by being willing to be involved in some of those contentious meetings that took place early on, I helped establish the fact that this was not a white person's takeover of Grady," he reflected recently. "It was just the right thing to do for the institution. This effort had broader-based support than just white businessmen. I like to think our family and my history in the city brought some credibility, that the Russells are, at the end of the day, looking to do the right thing for the city of Atlanta." Michael had skin in the game in a way that none of the rest of us could claim, and that made a difference.

The Detail Man

Tom Bell's contacts were also critical to the success of our efforts. In the beginning, his position on the Emory Healthcare Board gave him an entrée to the FDHA structure—Pam Stephenson and Dr. Chris Edwards, the chair and co-chair of their board—that enabled him to define and validate the problem. Through his Republican political contacts, he helped us connect with some of the commissioners from North Fulton County, other Northside Atlanta political leaders, and the suburban hospitals, who otherwise might not have been as sensitive to the urgency of the Grady issue. From his position on the Emory board, he was also able to convince Emory and Morehouse to be patient when it came to recouping the money owed for doctors' salaries, and to give us time to work out payment.

But I think Bell's major contribution was, as he says himself, "recognizing the problem in the first place, doing enough initial investigation to ensure that the problem was real—and then, not allowing nothing to happen." Bell was our detail man. He constantly pushed to clarify the problem and to keep the solution simple—and constantly reminded us of the consequences of doing nothing. He refused to take the initial "no" from the Chamber as a final answer, and pushed us by detailing the problem until we were willing to explore getting involved.

The Spear-catcher

From his very first conversation with Tom Bell, Pete Correll was a big part of what made this effort a success. For one thing, he knew how to use the cocktail hour. His meeting with Jimmy Williams resulted in a commitment that gave the task force incredible leverage when it came time to push for the institution of the 501(c)(3) board. Both the Woodruff Foundation's willingness to commit funds and their insistence on the board change before they did so helped make the point that without that change, Grady would have trouble getting access to private foundation money—and that was critical because it was clear that the existing combination of patient dollars and county funds was not going to be sufficient to run the hospital.

Correll functioned as our lightning rod—he called the role "spear-catcher." "If somebody throws spears, somebody's got to catch them," he says.

> I was at a unique point in my life. I no longer worked for a public company. I had built a reputation in Atlanta such that people knew I was at least trying to do the right thing, even if I may have done it in the wrong way. I got some ugly things said about me, but I was at a stage of my life where it didn't bother me very much. I think there weren't many people in our community at that moment who would have been comfortable taking that level of heat and pressure. I had spent a career running Georgia-Pacific so I was comfortable with the press and I was comfortable with adversarial situations. A change like this needed a figurehead, and I was able to play that role.

After our task force work was done, Correll told me, "The things that I had to do in that process would not have been possible had I been a sitting CEO of Georgia-Pacific Corporation." Picking your project leadership is a critical decision. When you are dealing with a controversial issue, you've got to pick someone whom the political powers and the demonstrators can't intimidate. Pete was the perfect guy.

All three of these "urban statesmen" have continued to be part of the Grady solution. The story you've read only skims the surface of their commitment to this institution and the difference they made in its survival. All three currently serve on the GMHC board—the 501(c)(3) board created based on the Greater Grady Task Force's recommendation. And that board was impressive. To help ensure Grady's long-term success, the new board of directors included well-known civic leaders, top CEOs, and highly respected African-American leaders such as Dr. Louis Sullivan, founder of Morehouse Medical School and former cabinet secretary. One business reporter told me that the board looked like a Fortune 500 slate.

Although the hospital still struggles financially, it has made tremendous strides both operationally and financially since the new board was put in place. The CEO hired by the new board in 2010, Michael Young, left in 2012 to return to his native Pennsylvania (Correll reminds me that it's not unusual for a transitional leader to have a short tenure), and the GMHC board then hired John Haupert from Parkland Health and Hospital System in Dallas, Texas—one of the hospitals our consultants looked to as an example of "best practices" for large safety-net hospitals. Grady is now recognized nationally for its turn-around success, including the additions of the new Correll Cardiac Center and the Bernie Marcus Stroke Center.

An additional factor contributing to the success of the Greater Grady Task Force was the support provided by the Metro Atlanta Chamber. We helped bring the right people into the room, made available the facts that helped define the problem and the solution, coordinated multiple consultants and an extensive fact-checking and legal research operation, promoted connectivity between business and political leaders, and managed media contacts. As Rick Stafford, former CEO of the Allegheny Conference in Pittsburgh and Distinguished Service Professor at Carnegie Mellon University's Heinz College School of Public Policy and Management, says, "Public policy change is a process that needs to be managed. It has many components. Leadership is the most important but it is not sufficient. Staff work is instrumental, and there has to be someone who can provide it."[23] The Metro Atlanta Chamber filled that role.

In March 2013, the Grady Health Foundation—the fund-raising arm of Grady Hospital—presented the Metro Atlanta Chamber with its Health Care Legacy Award and celebrated the reorganization of the hospital with a video called "The Grady Miracle." Correll, Bell, and Russell all had a role in the video, but the most prominently featured celebrant was the Rev. Tim McDonald, one of the most vocal opponents of the Greater Grady Task Force back in 2007. "I don't know of anything that I've been involved in that has brought me any more joy than where I see Grady now," he says in the video. "That did not come without a struggle. It did not happen without some misconceptions and some tension. It happened because the business community, the faith community, the political community came together.... It is the community at its best."[24]

The personal credibility of our two task force chairmen—one white and "disarmingly candid" and the other black with a long history in Atlanta's African-American community—along with the detail work of a third task force member with a determination to see change happen, were key components in what the Grady Hospital Foundation calls "The Grady Miracle."

Issues such as Oklahoma City's MAPS projects and the reorganization of Grady Hospital, which involve business executives working with local governing bodies, are typical for urban statesmen, but sometimes their work hits further up the line. In Salt Lake City, business executives took on an issue that required them to work with the state legislature as they attempted to speed up the implementation of a long-term transportation plan. Their story is next.

---

[23] Rick Stafford, interview, 13 January 2012.
[24] Grady Health Foundation, "The Grady Miracle," (video).

In Oklahoma City, the North Canadian River, pre-MAPS, was a low-volume channel that required mowing a couple of times a year. The unattractive river contributed to the city's image as a "dry and dusty hick town."

Courtesy of Greater Oklahoma City Chamber

Today's Oklahoma River, renamed due to the efforts of Ray Ackerman,
provides scenic vistas and an Olympic-class rowing venue.

Courtesy of Greater Oklahoma City Chamber

Oklahoma City's "Bricktown," prior to its renovation with MAPS funds, was an ordinary warehouse and manufacturing district.

Courtesy of Greater Oklahoma City Chamber

MAPS funded the construction of the Bricktown Canal, creating a
Riverwalk with restaurants and a shopping district.

Financial difficulties nearly closed Grady Hospital, Atlanta's medical safety net, in 2007, before a task force recommended and then implemented a new governance structure.

Courtesy of Metro Atlanta Chamber

Atlanta business executives Michael Russell, Tom Bell, and A.D. "Pete" Correll were the prime movers behind the efforts to save Grady Hospital.

Courtesy of Metro Atlanta Chamber

The Grady Task Force was controversial, and protests against the Metro Atlanta Chamber and the task force effort occurred so frequently the Chamber began greeting demonstrators with coffee and doughnuts.

Courtesy of Metro Atlanta Chamber

A dedicated sales tax referendum campaign lead by Salt Lake City business executives in 2006 resulted in multiple extensions to TRAX, Salt Lake City's light rail transit system.

Courtesy of Salt Lake Chamber

Lane Beattie, President and CEO of the Salt Lake Chamber, provided exceptional support for the urban statesmen championing the 2006 sale tax referendum.

Courtesy of Salt Lake Chamber

Scott Anderson, who led the 2015 Alliance, the Chamber-supported organization pushing for a transportation sales tax referendum, received the Salt Lake Chamber's "Giant in Our City" award in 2013, in recognition for his work on the referendum and other public policy endeavors.

Courtesy of Salt Lake Chamber

In 2009 in the wake of Hurricane Ike, Dr. Mae Jemison headed a task force of the Greater Houston Partnership focused on planning for and recovering from natural disasters. Here Dr. Jemison is shown is her previous capacity as a NASA Mission Specialist on Space Lab Japan. Dr. Jemison was also the first woman of color in space as a member of the crew of the Space Shuttle Endeavor.

Photo courtesy of NASA

Hurricane Ike, with winds extending 120 miles from the center and
damages exceeding fifty billion dollars, was the largest and costliest
hurricane ever to hit Texas, said the Governor's Commission for Disaster
Recovery and Renewal. The hurricane came ashore at Galveston on
September 13, 2008, and caused extensive flooding, power outages
and property damage throughout the Greater Houston area.

Photo © Houston Chronicle/Smiley N. Pool
Used with permission.

A series of dams on the Chattahoochee River at Columbus, Georgia,
altered the flow and appearance of the river prior to the demolition of
two of the dams in 2012 and 2013.

Courtesy of Marquette McKnight,
Media, Marketing and More! Inc., Columbus, Georgia

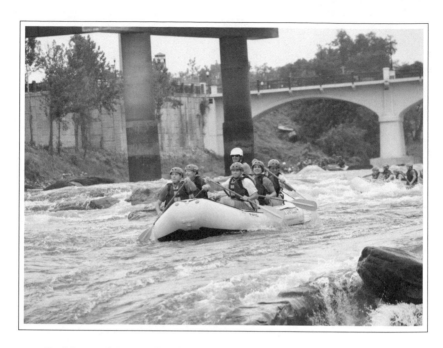

On Memorial Day weekend, 2013, Columbus, Georgia, celebrated the opening of the longest urban whitewater course in the world. Building the $24.4 million 2.5 mile course involved two state governments, two cities, the Army Corps of Engineers, and numerous federal, state, local, civic, and environmental organizations.

Courtesy of Marquette McKnight,
Media, Marketing and More! Inc., Columbus, Georgia

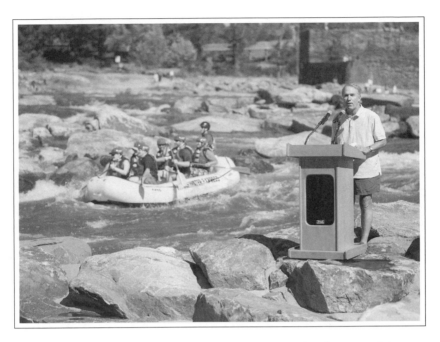

Columbus, Georgia business executive John Turner, who championed the whitewater project for fifteen years, speaks at the opening ceremonies.

Columbus, Georgia citizens gathered at the river's edge to celebrate the opening of the whitewater course.

Courtesy of Marquette McKnight,
Media, Marketing and More! Inc., Columbus, Georgia

5

Salt Lake City: Road Warriors[1]

A single, compelling policy issue can sometimes marshal a diverse group of leaders. In 2006, in Salt Lake City, Utah, transportation was such an issue. Consider the following cast of characters. Keith Rattie, former chairman and CEO of Questar and the 2006 chairman of the Salt Lake City Chamber of Commerce, is not a fan of taxes. "I'm one who personally does not believe every good plan deserves funding," he says. Clark Ivory, CEO of Ivory Homes, the number one homebuilder in the state of Utah, has made immigration reform his number one personal issue. Scott Anderson, president and CEO of Zions Bank, is a key figure in the USTAR program, an effort to use the science and technology products of Utah research institutions to grow in-state businesses. Lane Beattie does not meet our definition of an urban statesman—he's a paid professional policy man, a former president of the Utah State Senate and the current president and CEO of the greater Salt Lake City Chamber of Commerce—but he is a major player in the Salt Lake City business community. Despite their various backgrounds, interests, and priorities, these four men pulled together to deliver one of the most successful local transportation funding initiatives in the country—and an example of urban statesmanship at its most effective.

Beattie has an exceptional talent for working behind the scenes, energizing the folks out front and capitalizing on their expertise and

---

[1] Much of this chapter is based on interviews with the following participants: Lane Beattie, Keith Rattie, Scott Anderson, Clark Ivory, Scott Parson, Mark Howell, and Natalie Gochnour. Quotations from these sources will not be individually footnoted. Other sources will be documented as appropriate.

talent. Moving to the Chamber position after three years as liaison between the Utah Governor's Office and the Salt Lake Organizing Committee during the 2002 Winter Olympics and a long tenure in the state senate, Beattie was aware of both the issues and the politics affecting Utah's business community. The Chamber expected him to focus on economic development and promoting pro-business legislation.[2] With the able support of Salt Lake City's business leaders, he hit the ground running.

One of the first issues Beattie identified as critical to the Salt Lake City business community was transportation. During his time in the state senate, especially during the run-up to the Olympics, Utah had rebuilt I-15, the major interstate highway running through Salt Lake County, and constructed a light-rail transit system. But continued fast growth and increasing congestion had convinced Beattie that additional transportation improvements in the short term were necessary if the Salt Lake City economy were to continue to grow. Denver and Phoenix, frequent competitors with Salt Lake City for new businesses and conferences, had recently approved one-cent sales taxes to fund transit and were using the scheduled 2016 completion of their projects as a recruiting tool.[3] Regional planning agencies—the Wasatch Front Regional Council and the Mountainland Association of Governments—recognized the need for improvement and had developed long-range plans designed to meet transportation needs in 2030, including both transit and roads. The needs were extensive, potentially costing $30.5 billion. "We asked them how they planned to get the money," Beattie said. "They said their job was planning, not funding."

---

[2] Jennifer Nii, "Beattie to head S.L. [Salt Lake] Chamber," *Deseret News*, 28 May 2003, D10.

[3] Patty Henetz, "Big tax bump asked for TRAX fast track," *Salt Lake Tribune*, 20 April 2006, http://archive.sltrib.com/printfriendly.php?id=3729448&1type=NGPSID, accessed 9 July 2012.

Defining the Issue

The Chamber of Commerce decided to find a way to do both. They formed an internal group called the 2015 Alliance, "a business-led effort to accelerate transportation investment in Utah" in early 2006. As the name implies, the goal of the Alliance was to develop a funding plan to implement the 2030 goals fifteen years early.[4] Headed by Zions Bank president and CEO Scott Anderson and real estate developer Kem Gardner, chairman of The Gardner Company, the Alliance began its work by discussing transportation needs with the Utah Department of Transportation (UDOT) and the Utah Transit Authority (UTA). They then commissioned an independent study to examine the Salt Lake City area's current transportation needs and the impact of waiting until 2030 to implement the improvements identified by the planning agencies. Alliance members felt that the use of outside nationally prominent consultants would add weight and objectivity to their position. As Chamber chairman Rattie noted, although UDOT and UTA had relatively high credibility since they had recently completed major highway and transit projects on time and below budget for the 2002 Winter Olympics, "like most government agencies, they were regarded as parochial, bureaucratic, and tending to gold-plate their projects."

Scott Anderson delivered the results of the 2015 Alliance study to the community at a press conference on June 20. The consultants, HTNB Corporation and Tom Warne and Associates, reported that the Wasatch Front corridor had experienced population growth at a rate 2.5 times the national average during the decade between 1990 and 2000, and 75 percent of the growth was internal. Though recent improvements (especially those connected with the 2002 Olympics) had increased highway capacity by 12 percent, vehicle miles driven had increased by 66 percent, leading the Wasatch Front Range

---

[4] Utah 2015 Transportation Alliance, "Accelerating Utah Transportation Investments: Needs, Costs, Funding Options," 12 June 2006, 1. Hereafter referred to as "2015 Alliance Report."

Council to calculate that the average driver experienced 17 "annual delay hours" idling in traffic in 2001—a number that would triple by 2030.[5] The region's rapid growth, the study concluded, "is burdening the transportation infrastructure and threatening the region's economy and quality of life."[6]

While the Alliance study and the UDOT focused on time spent on the roads, the UTA was urging Gardner and Anderson to push for additional and early funding for the mass transit portions of the 2030 plans. Seeing needs broader than just increasing transit, Anderson said, "We told [the UTA] we would have to include all types of transportation, and they agreed."

The decision to include both highway and transit improvements in the initiative shaped the Alliance's message in important ways. "A big part of our success was our ability to present a holistic transportation solution including both roads and transit," Lane Beattie later reflected. "Any time we found ourselves getting too far in one camp or the other, the going got rough. The best policy and public communications strategy is to acknowledge and advocate the very real needs in both modes of transportation.... Focusing on one or the other is like asking which is more important, the gas pedal or the brake. Let's be honest; you've got to have both."[7] The total package addressed by the consultant's report listed ten highway projects, including extensive improvements to I-15 and construction of a new freeway, the Mountain View Corridor, and, on the transit side, construction of four new light rail (TRAX) extensions and expansion of the heavy commuter rail service (called Frontrunner), to connect Weber County in the north thorough Salt Lake City to Provo in Utah County in the south.[8]

---

[5] "2015 Alliance Report," 2.

[6] Ibid.

[7] Lane Beattie, speech, 5 September 2007. I received a copy of this speech, which was made to a civic organization in Boise, Idaho, from its author.

[8] "2015 Alliance Report," 3–4.

Also at issue was the timing of the proposed construction projects. In 2006 Utah was in line for significant federal funding for both transit and highway construction. Natalie Gochnour, who was then COO and chief spokesperson for the Chamber, says both UTA and UDOT were important in helping to convey a sense of urgency. "They helped us understand the window of opportunity that was available to us," she remembers. "They had good contacts with the federal government and good awareness of funding sources.... We were going to fall back about 15 spots in the federal funding line if we couldn't go after that money now."

The Alliance, capitalizing on its Chamber of Commerce base and coordinated by Beattie, deployed a number of business executives to spread the message that the transportation timetable needed to change. In addition to Anderson and Chamber chairman Keith Rattie, Clark Ivory (CEO of Ivory Homes), Scott Parson (president of Staker Parson and the Chamber's legislative affairs chairman), and Mark Howell (president of AmericanWest Bank) hit the circuit. The goal, Rattie said, was "taking the messaging away from the self-interested agencies [UTA and UDOT] and giving the initiative a business message." Ivory met with a variety of legislators. Anderson recalled, "We did lots of work with the media, with [other] chambers of commerce [in the region]; we held town hall meetings and rallies and sold 'hand bands'[9] and accepted public contributions."

The studies and the speakers served an important role in defining and clarifying the problem: Utah in general and Salt Lake County in particular were fast outgrowing their transportation systems. Convincing people of the need for improved transportation infrastructure, though, was the easy part of the campaign. The long, narrow Wasatch Valley lent itself to transit development, and the TRAX light rail system first authorized in 1997 had proved popular. By 2006 the light rail lines originally scheduled to move 21,000 daily

---

[9] He means those imprinted plastic wrist bracelets.

riders were carrying more than 55,000 riders each weekday.[10] North-south highway arteries were limited, so that an accident anywhere could cause an hours-long logjam. The idea of improving infrastructure, from a conceptual standpoint, was a relatively easy sell. The funding mechanism was the issue.

A Tale of Two Taxes

Separate from the campaign conducted by the 2015 Alliance, UTA approached the Salt Lake County Council with a request that the council float an $895 million bond issue (to be repaid through property taxes) to fund the early build-out of four TRAX lines included in the 2030 regional plan. While the bond issue required voter approval, the council had the authority to place it on the ballot without any additional legislative action. On July 18, the council voted 6-1 to place the item on the November 2006 ballot—with a caveat.[11] The Alliance, acting as the voice of the Chamber, was advocating a different funding proposal based on an incremental sales tax, and the council planned to replace the property tax proposal on the ballot with the Alliance's proposal if the legislature approved its use.

Not surprisingly, increased property tax as a funding mechanism had its detractors. The 2015 Alliance and others at the Chamber of Commerce advocated a different approach. The Chamber proposed funding the construction speed-up with a dedicated sales tax of up to one percent, implemented in quarter-cent increments. The sales tax, the Chamber argued, would generate more money while more equitably impacting business. County council members, like the business community, were concerned about the impact of a property tax increase on economic development. A Utah Foundation study

---

[10] Beattie, speech, 5 September 2007.

[11] Derek P. Jensen, "TRAX is on track to arrive on ballot," *Salt Lake Tribune*, 18 July 2006, http://archive.sltrib.com/printfriendly.php?id=4064557&itype=NGPSID, accessed 16 July 2012.

released in late August noted that businesses would pay 43 percent of the property tax assessment, but only a third of the sales tax.[12] Additionally, in spite of the differential impact, the study concluded, voters would likely prefer a sales tax increase because it would be "incremental, easier to pay, and wouldn't provoke sticker shock the way annual property tax notices do."[13]

While the UTA (property tax) proposal applied only to Salt Lake County, and only to transit, the Alliance/Chamber proposal allowed any county in the state to place a sales tax designated for transportation (up to one cent, in ¼-cent increments) on its ballot, and extended the reach of the projects to be funded by the tax to include roads. Such a structure, argued Keith Rattie and other Chamber spokespersons, would encourage regional planning with regard to both highway improvement and transit development. The *Salt Lake City Tribune*, while it preferred the speed with which the bond issue could proceed, acknowledged that "[the sales tax] would raise more money, and it would provide not only building capital but operating funds, which the UTA will need to run the new trains. It also encompasses more projects, including commuter rail in Utah County, which would be a necessary alternative to the freeway when I-15 is rebuilt there."[14]

Unfortunately, the county council did not have the authority to place a sales tax increase for transit on the ballot. That authority had to come from the state legislature, and getting such a proposal on the November 2006 ballot would require the governor to call the legislature into special session. The Salt Lake County Council agreed

---

[12] Glen Warchol, "Huntsman is lobbying for special tax session," *Salt Lake Tribune*, 2 September 2006, http://archive.sltrib.com/printfriendly.php?id =4278343&itype=NGPSID, accessed 12 July 2012.

[13] Ibid.

[14] "Bond for TRAX: Of two plans, this will get the job done sooner," *Salt Lake Tribune*, 24 June 2006, http://archive.sltrib.com/printfriendly.php?id= 3973877&itype=NGPSID, accessed 12 July 2012.

to substitute the sales tax initiative for the property tax increase should the legislature approve it in special session.[15]

So as of 18 July 2006, the business community of Salt Lake City, represented by the Chamber of Commerce and its spokesmen under the umbrella of the 2015 Alliance, faced three challenges: they had to sell the governor on calling a special session which included consideration of their sales tax proposal; they had to convince the legislature to place the sales tax proposal on the ballot; and, once the proposal was on the ballot, they had to sell the sales tax proposal to the citizens of Salt Lake County—all by November 7.

A Special Session

The general session of the 2006 Utah legislature had ended on 1 March 2006, with substantial business still on the table. An income tax reform proposal touted by Governor Jon Huntsman, Jr., had been approved by the Senate but gutted by the House in the waning hours of the session. Huntsman indicated almost immediately following the end of the forty-five-day general session that he intended to call a special session later in the year to deal with the matter.[16]

As the spring progressed, the Chamber of Commerce transportation proposals began to take shape. Chamber leaders knew their preferred funding mechanism, a local option sales tax, needed legislative authorization. The next general session of the legislature would not convene until January 2007, meaning that the tax could not be approved by voters before November 2007. However, if the sales tax authority could be included on a special-session agenda, the tax question could be placed on the November 2006 ballot, speeding up the process by a year and removing the one obvious advantage of the bond issue/property tax proposal (which could be placed on the

---

[15] Jensen, "TRAX is on track to arrive on ballot," 18 July 2006.

[16] Glen Warchoal, "Tax overhaul top issue for special session," *Salt Lake Tribune*, 3 March 2006, http://archive.sltrib.com/printfriendly.php?id=3564846&itype=NGPSID, accessed 9 July 2012.

ballot without any additional legislative consideration) as well as improving the position of Utah in the federal transportation funding queue.[17]

The governor and the legislature initially resisted the Chamber's request, through Scott Anderson and the 2015 Alliance, to place the sales-tax issue on a special-session agenda, arguing that the issue was too complex to be decided in a one-day special session. The Chamber pushed back. CEO Lane Beattie responded, "We are not asking them to debate taxes. We are only asking them to allow the citizens of Utah to vote if they would like to have increased transportation services by increasing a small portion of the sales tax on a county-by-county basis."[18] On June 26, the Salt Lake County Council joined the Chamber in its call for a special session.[19]

Governor Huntsman remained reluctant, saying on June 29 that he had no plans "to do anything now" but might consider a referendum to measure public opinion on how to meet transportation needs in the future.[20] Through a spokesman, he did indicate a willingness to "discuss the special session proposal with legislators and…review a lengthy report detailing the transportation crisis prepared by the alliance."[21] Other legislators, including Senator Sheldon Killpack, co-

---

[17] "Bond for TRAX: Of two plans, this will get the job done sooner," 24 June 2006.

[18] Paul Beebe, "Senators: Special session no place to talk tax hike," *Salt Lake Tribune*, 23 June 2006, http://archive.sltrib.com/printfriendly.php?id=3970644&itype=NGPSID, accessed 9 July 2012.

[19] "County Council urges special session," *Salt Lake Tribune*, 29 June 2006, http://archive.sltrib.com/printfriendly.php?id=3992677&itype=NGPSID, accessed 9 July 2012.

[20] Patty Henetz, "Majority backs bond to speed TRAX lines," *Salt Lake Tribune*, 30 June 2006, http://archive.sltrib.com/printfriendly.php?id=3997472&itype=NGPSID, accessed 12 July 2012.

[21] Beebe, "Senators: Special session no place to talk tax hike," 23 June 2006.

chair of the Transportation Interim Committee, argued for waiting until the next regular legislative session to consider the issue.[22]

Increasing pressure on the governor and the legislature was the fact that public support for the early completion of the transportation system was overwhelming. One UTA poll indicated that 90 percent of Utah voters wanted to see the transportation issue on the ballot. A *Salt Lake City Tribune* poll indicated that 60 percent of voters would vote to approve the bond issue/property-tax proposal. Questioned informally, voters reacted even more enthusiastically to the idea of a sales-tax option.[23] The polls, combined with the Salt Lake County Council's July 18 vote to place the bond issue on the ballot with a provision to substitute a sales tax if the legislature approved it, and a Utah County decision to place a previously authorized transportation sales tax on the ballot, made clear that voters considered the transportation issue both pressing and popular.[24]

Concurrently, Governor Huntsman was negotiating a complex deal for income tax reduction with the legislature—and in order to pass the reforms before the November elections (allowing incumbent

---

[22] Henetz, "Majority backs bond to speed TRAX lines," 30 June 2006.

[23] Jensen, "TRAX is on track to arrive on ballot," 18 July 2006.

[24] Todd Hollingshead, "Utah County puts transit tax on ballot," *Salt Lake Tribune*, 1 August 2006, http://archive.sltrib.com/printfriendly.php?id= 4121961&itype=NGPSID, accessed 12 July 2012. Utah County's situation was complicated. Unlike Salt Lake County, Utah County had not yet used all of the half-cent sales tax available to counties for transportation previously authorized by the legislature. They decided to place the previously authorized sales tax referendum on the ballot in 2006 because they needed access to mass transit while portions of Interstate 15 running through Utah County were being rebuilt. The *Salt Lake City Tribune* reported on 22 October 2006 that, "The Utah Department of Transportation hopes to begin rebuilding Interstate 15 through the county by 2013 if money can be found to do so. The county has no other north-south traffic arteries. Unless it gets rail service to get commuters out of their cars, I-15 will slow to a near-halt, bottling up travel and commerce on one of the nation's most important transportation corridors."

legislators to use the tax relief as a campaign issue), he needed to call a special session in September. As Huntsman traveled the state drumming up support for his compromise tax measure, Chamber chairman Rattie endorsed Huntsman's proposal, noting it would "move Utah from the 13th highest income tax rate in the nation to the 11th lowest," a change that would "make Utah more competitive in attracting top executives and, by extension, their companies."[25]

In the midst of the income-tax campaign, Anderson and Beattie met with Governor Huntsman to press the business case for the transportation sales tax. It was important to Huntsman to know that the legislature would not leave him hanging if he included the proposal in his call for a special session; Beattie and Anderson had met with legislative leaders and were able to give him that assurance. By the end of the hour-long meeting, Anderson says, they were able to convince the governor "that the business community was really serious, that they would provide [political] cover [to both the governor and the legislative leaders], that they would do the advertising to get the initiative passed by the people, and that they would...remember and, you know, reward those who were friendly. So...when the governor said, 'I'll do it,' [the legislative leaders] said, 'We'll bring our bodies along.' But they really were insistent that the business community lead it and that we would have the resources to be able to run a campaign that would let it win."

Since a special session appeared to be imminent, the governor agreed to have both House and Senate Republican caucuses—possessing a super majority in both legislative houses, they were the only caucuses that mattered—consider whether to include the 2015 Alliance/Chamber sales tax proposal on the special-session agenda. The Utah House endorsed including the measure on the special-session agenda, but the Senate balked, saying that, "the bill had too

---

[25] Warchol, "Huntsman is lobbying for special tax session," 2 September 2006.

many unanswered questions."[26] The Chamber indicated that it would continue an aggressive lobbying campaign. "We have the support of the governor's office," Chamber spokeswoman Natalie Gochnour said. "When senators have more information, they will be inclined to support the sales tax option."[27] Rattie identifies Scott Anderson as being particularly effective at this stage of the negotiation. "Scott was very effective with key members of the legislature," he said. "He has a very low-key, self-effacing way of convincing the guy across the table that the change Scott is advocating was the other guy's idea."

When the governor issued a call for a special session on September 15, the sales-tax issue was included. The bill that emerged from the session on September 19, known as "Proposition 3," contained a restriction not in the Alliance's original proposal: one fourth of the money collected had to be used to buy land for future road and transit projects. The practical effect of the change was that, if the sales tax initiative were to be approved in the November election, rather than building the four light rail lines envisioned in the original proposal, UTA would build three lines. The remaining funds would be used to acquire right-of-way for either extending the heavy commuter rail into Utah County or extending the Mountain View Corridor highway—both goals of the 2015 Alliance proposal.

On the Ballot

Rattie, Anderson, and the rest of the 2015 Alliance crew—again supported by Beattie—then had a little more than six weeks to ensure

---

[26] Senate President John Valentine, quoted in Patty Henetz and Glen Warchol, "Alliance still pushes transit sales tax hike," *Salt Lake Tribune*, 7 September 2006, http://archive.sltrib.com/printfriendly.php?id=4298710&itype=NGPSID, accessed 12 July 2012.

[27] Patty Henetz and Glen Warchol, "Alliance still pushes transit sales tax hike," *Salt Lake Tribune*, 7 September 2006, http://archive.sltrib.com/printfriendly.php?id=4298710&itype=NGPSID, accessed 12 July 2012.

that the public would pass the tax measure. Luckily they were not starting from scratch. Much of the campaign to raise awareness about the transportation issue in general and to lobby for a special legislative session had been conducted in the media, so the public was already aware of both the problem and the proposal to solve it. The 2015 Alliance, working from its Chamber of Commerce base, had also planned for success. "We had already done our research and had engaged a marketing group and had a campaign ready to go," Anderson reported. "We did lots of public media and educational events when we were trying to get the Governor to call the special session."

With the sales tax proposal now on the ballot, the campaign kicked into high gear. Only weeks away from the election, the Chamber targeted its fund-raising campaign at those who stood to benefit from the increased transportation spending: construction and equipment contractors in the road and rail sector. When the first financial disclosures were reported six days before the election, more than half of the almost $524,000 collected had come from construction and equipment companies.[28] The strategy was deliberate, Rattie said: "[The Chamber] went to the major construction groups and told them that since they stood to benefit and we were in a time bind, we needed their support." Alliance member Scott Parson, whose business, Staker Parson, was a paving and construction company, was particularly effective as a fundraiser.

The Chamber of Commerce, though, did not stand alone in supporting the initiative. By the end of October, Proposition 3 had been endorsed by the governor, both senators, all three congressional representatives, both the Salt Lake County Republican and Democratic Party chairs, most of the mayors in the county, both major newspapers, the anti-poverty group Utah Issues, and the Sierra

---

[28] Patty Henetz, "Transit firms give big to back Prop. 3," *Salt Lake Tribune*, 1 November 2006, http://archive.sltrib.com/printfriendly.php?id=4583803&itype=NGPSID, accessed 9 July 2012.

Club.[29] Rattie attributes this broad-based support to the balance between transit and roads in the transportation plan and the business-based approach to defining the issues. "The *Tribune* had supported environmental issues and favored transit so we got a strong endorsement from them," he said. "Bob Bennett and Orrin Hatch, our Senators, and our three Representatives met with business leaders and read our study and got on board when Governor Huntsman, state legislators, and the business community gave them cover on the tax issue. There were lots of good opinion pieces in the papers." Also important to the campaign, Rattie said, was that "in the weeks prior we put the business community out there instead of the politicians and that generated widespread public support." Jim Bennett, head of the "Vote for 3" campaign, observed in a *Tribune* editorial: "All of the groups rarely agree on anything, yet all of them are united in support of Proposition 3...."[30]

On November 7, Proposition 3 won 64 percent of the vote. "The message here," opined the *Tribune*, "is that, though Utahns are fiscal conservatives, they will support tax increases when they agree that there is a demonstrated need. The state's leaders have done a good job of publicizing the transportation-funding crisis; they have been less willing to raise taxes to solve it. But with Proposition 3, the County Council stole a march on the Legislature and took decisive action, which voters endorsed overwhelmingly on Tuesday."[31]

---

[29] Jim Bennett, "A vote for Proposition 3 is a vote for Utah's future," *Salt Lake Tribune*, 29 October 2006, http://archive.sltrib.com/printfriendly. php?id=4567858&itype=NGPSID; Patty Henetz, "Transportation proposition backed by congressional delegation," *Salt Lake Tribune*, 31 October 2006, http://archive.sltrib.com/printfriendly.php?id=4578814&itype=NGPSID; and "Tax boost for transit gets big thumbs up," *Salt Lake Tribune*, 7 November 2006, http://archive/sltrib.com/printfriendly.php?id=4618531&itype= NGP-SID (all accessed 9 July 2012).

[30] Bennett, "A vote for Proposition 3 is a vote for Utah's future," 29 October 2006.

[31] "Props send message: Voters will support tax increases for transportation," *Salt Lake Tribune*, 9 November 2006, http://archive.sltrib.

Outcomes

Six years later, the success of the initiative is obvious. Two of the light rail (TRAX) extensions funded by the sales tax initiative—the West Valley City and mid-Jordan lines—opened in 2011. A line to the Salt Lake City International Airport opened in April 2013, and the final line, south to Draper, opened in August 2013. Construction on the FrontRunner commuter rail line south to Provo through Utah County is underway.[32] As for the two major projects impacted by the initiative on the highway side, the rebuilding of I-15 in Utah County was completed in an unprecedented 35 months, and land acquisition and construction on the Mountain View Corridor is well underway.[33] An interesting side note: all of this construction has occurred during the administration of Mayor Ralph Becker, a strong transportation advocate who was serving in the legislature at the time the sales tax initiative was authorized, and who made sure the system was built as envisioned.

"This all happened because the business community stepped up and took control of this project," says Lane Beattie. The reason for such success, he said in a speech to a Boise, Idaho, business organization, on 5 September 2007, was both clear and simple:

> Collaboration wins every time. We always achieve more when we work together. With Proposition 3, several components contributed to our successful collaboration. We had a shared problem of traffic congestion that was threatening our economic performance. We had a

---

com/printfriendly.php?id=4625658&itype=NGPSID, accessed 9 July 2012.

[32] "Airport TRAX Line Community Celebration," http://www/rideuta.com/uploads/Press Release04122013.pdf, accessed 24 March 2014; "Draper TRAX extension grand opening," http://rideuta.com/uploads/PressRelease08162013.pdf, accessed 24 March 2014; "Frontlines 2015," http://rideuta.copm/mc/?page=projects-Frontline2015, accessed 24 March 2014.

[33] For current information on the status of Mountain View corridor projects, visit http://www.udot.utah.gov/projects/f?p=250:3100:0::NO:3100, accessed 24 March 2014.

convener of stature in the form of a business community that was very willing to take the lead and force a policy decision with our elected leaders and the public. We had committed leaders in the form of key local government officials and businessmen. We had a clearly defined purpose to accelerate transportation investment. And finally, we had a common information base, provided by our independent study.[34]

Additionally, the initiative benefited from the collaboration between Lane Beattie and an impressive collection of Salt Lake City CEOs. Neither would have been successful without the other. Beattie, a skilled political operative with the weight of the Chamber behind him, had connections and an incredible understanding of Utah's political landscape. ("Every time I tried to find him," says Chamber COO Natalie Gochnour, "he'd be out roaming the state. He'd drive two and a half hours each way for a twenty-minute meeting with a dentist from western Utah who was a part-time legislator.") But former Senate presidents who have been out of office for several years only have so much power. It took the business executives like Rattie, Anderson, Howell, Ivory, and Parson, with their objective, fact-based, rational approach to give the needed heft to the transportation issue.

On the other hand, this talented group of CEOs would likely have been ineffective without Beattie's guidance. I asked a group of Salt Lake City businessmen what they did to assure passage of the sales-tax referendum. "Whatever Lane asked us to do," they told me. "And what was that?" "Make phone calls and write checks that don't bounce," said Scott Parson.

The combination of credibility and political savvy carried the day.

---

[34] Beattie, speech, 5 September 2007.

6

Houston: After the Storm[1]

Dr. Mae Jemison likes a challenge. Over the course of her career she has flown in space as the first woman astronaut of color on the Space Shuttle Endeavor, managed a healthcare program and conducted medical research for the Peace Corps in West Africa, started her own technology development and marketing firm, and served as both a spokesperson for and practitioner of improved science education. [2] She is the 2012 recipient of a half-million-dollar federal grant for the 100 Year Starship Project, whose mission is "to make sure all the capabilities needed to mount a human interstellar mission exist." [3] With that background, where is the challenge in running a task force for the Greater Houston Partnership?

It was, Jemison says, "like herding cats." The fact that the task force focused on the costliest hurricane in Texas history might have had something to do with that.

Jemison, then a member of the board of directors of the Greater Houston Partnership (GHP), was tapped to head a Disaster Planning and Recovery Task Force in response to a request from Texas

---

[1]A large part of the content of this chapter comes from interviews conducted in 2011 and 2012 with then Greater Houston Partnership president and CEO Jeff Moseley and the following Disaster Planning and Recovery Task Force Participants: Dr. Mae Jemison, Elaine Barber, Francisco Sanchez, and Joni Baird. While I will not identify their comments with separate footnotes, other sources will be so cited as appropriate.

[2] Mae Jemison, *Find Where the Wind Goes: Moments From My Life* (New York: Scholastic Press, 2001).

[3] Jeremy Hsu, "100-Year Starship Project, Led by Ex-Astronaut Mae Jemison, Sets Sights on Distant Stars," *Innovation News Daily*, 21 May 2012, http://www.huffingtonpost.com/2012/05/21/100-year-starship-project-mae-jemison-stars_n_1908922.html, accessed 23 May 2012.

Governor Rick Perry to GHP President and CEO Jeff Moseley. In September 2008, following a disastrous hurricane season (three hurricanes and a tropical storm hit the Texas coast), Perry created the Commission for Disaster Recovery and Renewal, tasked with working with local communities to help them rebuild, improve their ability to recover from future disasters, and seek federal assistance to help with recovery. When the commission generated its preliminary report in January 2009, Perry, looking for input from the business community in the affected area before issuing final recommendations, turned to Moseley, a former member of his staff, [4] for feedback. The GHP's board responded to the governor's request by appointing a task force charged with reviewing the report and generating its own recommendations.

An Obvious Choice

To Moseley, the choice of Jemison to head the task force was an obvious one: "She has outstanding credentials—she's a medical doctor, an astronaut, and an entrepreneur—so she has high credibility. People were willing to serve [on a task force] with such a leader," Moseley said. "She also has tremendous organizational skills, and is willing to move toward a decision." To Jemison, the assignment seemed to be a good fit. She was interested in science and environmental issues and had previously worked with Moseley on other committees and boards. "Also," she remembers, "I'm outgoing, so I covered a number of bases—logistics plus science plus being a people person.... I think it was this range of activities that led them to ask me to chair the task force."

Jemison's credibility and reputation simplified the task of recruiting the task force—a responsibility specifically delegated to the chair. Elaine Barber, a task force member and Vice President for Public Policy at GHP, observed, "She knew who all the right people

---

[4] Moseley had served in several economic development positions in the Perry administration between 1999 and 2005, when he came to GHP.

were, and could get all the right people to the table. She did the phone calls and the due diligence on members. Her stature—the request coming from her—made them willing to serve."

Recruiting the task force was the easy part of the job. Jemison's work leading the group was complicated both by the severity of the disaster it addressed and the complexity of the response that it required.

The Costliest Storm

Hurricane Ike was not the strongest hurricane ever to hit the Texas coast, but it was the most expensive. And given the history of hurricanes in Texas, Ike had big shoes to fill.

In 1900, an unnamed storm, described in harrowing detail in Erik Larson's 2000 book *Isaac's Storm*, struck Galveston, killing eight thousand citizens—more than 20 percent of Galveston's population. Often called "The Great Storm," that hurricane remains the deadliest natural disaster to strike the US to date.[5]

In 2005, less than a month after Hurricane Katrina devastated the Gulf Coast and nearly destroyed the city of New Orleans, Hurricane Rita came calling. Classified as a Category 5 storm as it approached the Texas coast, Rita precipitated the largest coastal evacuation in the history of the country. Nearly three million people exited the city of Houston before the storm, downgraded by then to a Category 3, shifted course and made landfall at the Texas-Louisiana border on September 25, sparing the city a direct hit.[6]

The evacuation planning that resulted from Rita was good preparation for the 2008 hurricane season, when, in less than two

---

[5] Governor's Commission for Disaster Recovery and Renewal, Final Report (January 2010) 5.

[6] "In Receding Floodwaters, More Damage Found," MSNBC.com, 27 May 2005, http://www.msnbc.msn.com/id/9389157/ns/us_news-katrina_the_long_road_back/t/receding-floodwaters-more-damage-found/, accessed 21 May 2012.

months, Texas was hit by tropical storm Edouard and three hurricanes: Dolly, Gustav, and Ike.[7] The last of these, Hurricane Ike, was the worst. Classified as "only" a Category 2 storm, Ike was more than 400 miles wide, creating a devastating storm surge when it came ashore at Galveston on 13 September 2008. "With wind bands extending 120 miles from the center, recorded high water marks of 19 feet, and damages exceeding $50 billion, Hurricane Ike was likely the physically largest and costliest hurricane ever to hit Texas," reported the Governor's Commission for Disaster Recovery and Renewal. "It also may prove to be the second costliest hurricane in US history, behind only Hurricane Katrina.[8]

The area that sustained this damage was both geographically extensive and governmentally diverse. Harris County, in which Houston is located, "includes 34 cities, 125 law enforcement agencies, 54 fire departments, all sorts of non-profits who work with disasters (such as Red Cross and United Way, for example), and the folks who run the ship channel, and they all deal with emergencies," said Francisco Sanchez, a task-force member who represented the Harris County judge (the chief executive of Harris County) on the GHP task force. The Greater Houston Partnership comprises businesses in a ten-county area, including Galveston, which took Ike's initial hit.

Defining the Mission

Gathering a group that adequately represented all of these entities was Jemison's first task. "We needed people from the medical center, from the oil and gas industry, from the major geographical areas (the ten counties the Partnership covers), from infrastructure, from small business, and from the various governments. There were agencies

---

[7] Governor's Commission for Disaster Recovery and Renewal, Preliminary Report (26 March 2009) 10, in Governor's Commission for Disaster Recovery and Renewal (Texas), "Final Report to Governor Rick Perry," (January 2010).

[8] Governor's Commission (Texas), "Final Report," 6.

already responsible for disaster relief that already had plans in place. Our big issue needed to be, 'What unique perspective can business bring?'" Jemison reflects. "I saw our task as identifying what would allow business to come back faster—not so much what would save citizens but what would prevent economic damage. There were other agencies looking out for citizens." The resulting eighteen-person task force included representatives of area governments, non-profits, universities, hospitals, and a variety of businesses. Additional experts were invited in to address specific topics.

The time pressure created by the governor's request for a quick turn-around made responding to the Commission report the task force's most urgent priority, but the task force generally, and Jemison in particular, felt the group's mission should be broader. At the first meeting of the group on 12 February 2009, the task force adopted a purpose statement that included a responsibility to "develop and implement a restoration needs assessment and future planning process...assemble regional damage and recovery data...[and] define and quantify future disaster avoidance initiatives for the region..." in addition to responding to the governor's request.[9]

Looking back, members wondered whether this expansion of mission received the wholehearted commitment of the group, and whether broadening the task might have been a mistake. Elaine Barber, GHP's vice president for public policy, observed, "When we expanded [our mission] beyond [responding to the governor's report], we needed more buy-in from the task force. People were busy, and once they were finished with the governor's report they were ready to be done." Francisco Sanchez, frustrated by the number of business people who drifted away before the work was completed, concurred: "We were here to help them and towards the end we just

---

[9] "Mission Statement: Disaster Recovery and Planning Task Force," provided by Elaine Barber, Vice President for Public Policy, Greater Houston Partnership.

lost them…. It seems like the ones who had the most to gain were the ones who left the table."

Leading the Way

Jemison's skills as an organizer, consensus-builder, and facilitator were, in large part, responsible for the smooth functioning of the task force. She was, says Elaine Barber, very well prepared, and spent hours getting specifics ready for meetings. Jemison saw such preparation as one of her major contributions. "We had our hands on lots of reports from after Katrina and Rita, and there was a PBS special on Katrina three years later. I actually used clips from that program about the aftermath of Katrina at the opening meeting of the task force. So I gathered as much information as possible and sent it out before we met. I saw part of my job as digesting the information and then asking people to respond."

She organized the task force into three work groups: a Business Strategies Group, headed by Joni Baird, public and government affairs manager at Chevron, to identify strategies and best practices for developing disaster plans; an Infrastructure Group, headed by Leonard Waterworth, president and CEO of Dannenbaum Engineering, to study transportation (especially related to evacuation), building codes, and hardening infrastructure against future disasters; and a Resources Group headed by Anna Babin, president and CEO of United Way of Greater Houston, to define the resources businesses required during and immediately following a disaster and sources for providing them. Task-force members were divided among the groups; the leaders of the work groups were also empowered to bring in outside experts as necessary.[10]

The work groups met, usually by conference call, twice a month, and the task force as a whole came together for a meeting at the GHP offices monthly. Elaine Barber, as the representative of the sponsoring

---

[10] Information on the structure of the task force was provided by Elaine Barber, Vice President, Public Policy, Greater Houston Partnership.

agency, was tasked with sitting in on the telephone conferences of the sub-groups, keeping Jemison up-to-date on their discussions, and taking and circulating minutes of the general meetings. Jemison assigned each work group sections of the Governor's Report and charged them with reacting and developing recommendations to send back to the larger group for discussion and approval. "The first couple of meetings were actually sort of venting sessions—just getting issues out on the table," remembers Francisco Sanchez, who served on both the Business Strategy and Resources work groups. "Then we narrowed things down from this buffet of issues. We kept asking: What can we put on the plate that's manageable? What are the most significant issues? How can we address as many significant issues as possible? What will give us the most bang for the buck? It was a matter of setting priorities."

Jemison pushed the groups to conclusions, asking them to determine: "Here are the major important things. Here's why that's important. Here's generally what we need to do." In addition, she emphasized the need for all task-force members to be open to a wide range of ideas. She had, she says, "no particular place I wanted to run" when it came to recommendations, so "my strategy was to try to be as objective as possible—to acknowledge biases and put them on the table and talk about them." Her attitude was contagious. Sanchez recalls: "Everyone was very open about what the issues were. We knew from the beginning that all issues were valid (as far as being on the table) so everyone was very open about identifying issues. We were all looking for broader issues that had the most impact." Jemison considered such openness a matter of respect for the time and talents of the people she'd asked to become involved in the effort. She observes, "You are asking for their time, energy and passion; you must also let them volunteer their ideas."

Consensus Reached

The Business Strategies Group quickly reached a consensus on the crucial issue in their area: the need for a critical communications network linking businesses with government and other quasi-public entities (utilities, for instance) to promote business continuity and recovery. "One of our findings was the businesses needed better information and more capacity to talk with each other—both the big guys and the mom-and-pops," says Sanchez. "With medium to small businesses, each day they are closed beyond the first four or five days increases exponentially the risk of business failure. They need information to make decisions—for instance, from the power company: Which area will they be addressing next, and in what order will they restore lines? The same thing [was needed] with telecom and cable and with utility districts. How do we manage to get information from the public to the private sector?"

Baird, who chaired the work group, approached the same issue from a private sector perspective: "We needed a way to let businesses [and public agencies] make and communicate their plans with one another in advance of everything going public—so that, for instance, bus schedules could be synchronized if a business needed to close." Baird admits this particular item was, and still is, high on her personal disaster preparedness agenda, and that she asked to be put on the task force so she could push it. Clearly, she was not alone in her conviction.

Both Baird and Sanchez saw the communication issue as an opportunity for public-private cooperation. "Business had to be serious about doing their own planning, but what they needed from the government to make their plans work was information," Sanchez concluded. "We need to give them information to use in planning and then information to help them execute their plans during a disaster. They are responsible for continuity—we have to give them the real-time resources to enable that."

Two recommendations in the final GHP task force report drew on the work of the Business Strategies work group. Recommendation No.4 in the GHP report, titled "Develop critical businesses network," advocated improved and extensive communication between state and local governments and service providers and business—particularly small- and medium-sized businesses that were less likely to have comprehensive disaster plans. "Employers need to know as early as possible when highways and roads will close, if schools are closing, when evacuation warnings are sent and if they need to remain open to provide critical services to evacuees. Likewise, public officials and government agencies needs to know the conditions of business operations to enable them to better manage the disaster situation," the task force argued.[11]

The task force also advocated the use of local businesses to help with disaster relief and recovery wherever possible.[12] "Utilizing local service speeds the recovery process tremendously," the report declared. "For example, an open small, local trucking company that has a contingency contract with the City of Houston can haul debris sooner than a larger out-of-state trash-removal organization; and this increases the likelihood that the Texas business will survive."[13] Consistent with this emphasis on improved communication, Recommendation No.5, "Promote business continuity and emergency preparedness," argued for extending disaster planning, particularly to those small and medium-sized businesses that were weak in that area.[14]

---

[11] Greater Houston Partnership Disaster Planning and Recovery Task Force, "Recommendations to the Governor's Commission for Disaster Recovery and Renewal (10 June 2009) 10.

[12] Ibid., 9.

[13] Ibid., 10–11.

[14] Ibid., 12–14.

Herding Cats

While "herding the cats" of the Business Strategies work group proved fairly simple, Jemison's task with the Infrastructure group proved considerably more complicated. Most of the projects captured under this heading were both technically complex and extremely expensive, and the members of the group were generally people with strong technical backgrounds, stronger opinions, and little time for meetings.

Leonard Waterworth, president and CEO of Dannenbaum Engineering, who chaired the group, was, for example, a strong advocate for a project called the "Ike Dike." The "Dike," a 17-foot-high, 60-mile-long extension of the sea wall built after the 1900 no-name hurricane, was proposed by William Merrell, chair of marine sciences at Texas A&M University at Galveston. The idea, according to a *Wall Street Journal* article, was that the wall "would straddle the narrow entrance to Galveston Bay with 1,000-foot-long floodgates, allowing access to the city's port in good weather, but swinging shut when a storm approached to block floodwaters," which caused most of the hurricane damage. A similar system was in place in Rotterdam, Netherlands; another was nearing completion in St. Petersburg, Russia. [15]

The Ike Dike was quite controversial. Beachfront property owners and the Environmental Defense Fund were opposed, and some researchers argued the Dike might trap water behind it, making flooding worse. Cost was also an issue; conservative estimates placed the price tag at two to four billion dollars, and it was not at all clear that federal money would be available to support the construction,

---

[15] Ben Casselman, "Planning the 'Ike Dike' Defense—Houston-area Leaders Envision a 60-mile Barrier Against Hurricane Flooding," *Wall Street Journal*, 4 June 2009, A-3.

which was estimated to take ten years.[16] But Waterworth, who had come to his position at Dannenbaum after more than three years as commander of the Galveston Engineering District of the Army Corps of Engineers and was well-versed on the issues involved, was strongly in favor, and pushed for the work group to approve a recommendation for the Ike Dike based on his expertise.

The work group pushed back. Although they sent forward a recommendation for the Ike Dike, back-channel communication with Jemison led her to believe that support for the Dike within the work group was less than enthusiastic. One task force participant remembered: "Len Waterworth was very busy at the time and it was hard to get him to call meetings. It was hard to get him to give much time to the care and feeding, so to speak, of his committee, so they didn't fully understand the pros and cons of the issue." When questions regarding cost, feasibility, and workability of the structure came up, he wasn't always there to answer them. The result was disagreement at both the working-group level and at the task-force level about whether to recommend the Dike.

Jemison went to work. First, given the cost and complexity of the infrastructure projects under their review, she pushed the task force to establish a standard for comparing and evaluating the projects. They concluded: "Because these types of infrastructure projects require considerable funding at the state and federal levels to construct and maintain, governmental agencies and emergency management organizations need to understand fully the scope of such projects. What needs to be protected or saved? How can it be

---

[16] See the *Wall Street Journal* article, cited above, as well as two articles written by Ike Dike proponent William Merrell and published in the *Houston Chronicle* ("State needs 'Ike Dike' to avoid storm damage," 24 May 2009, and "Why the 'Ike Dike' is still a good idea," 2 May 2010) for more discussion of the pros and cons of the project.

done? How much will it cost? What is the impact [of] the implementation or non-implementation of various projects?"[17]

The task force then asked for and gathered opinions on those questions as they applied to the Ike Dike. The discussion, Barber said, "was very respectful. [Leonard Waterworth] reported and there were a number of very thoughtful, respectful questions. 'We've identified some issues about which we need some additional information,' was the tone. It was not negative. Dr. Jemison played a big role in that. She always knew the right questions to ensure than every position got a hearing." Discussion made it clear that there was no consensus on the project. By common consent, said Sanchez, "areas where there was no consensus were taken off the table."

The Ike Dike was only one of several large-scale projects brought before this working group. Other members proposed building or rebuilding roadways—the Blue Water Highway out of Galveston and the Grand Parkway out of Houston got particular attention—and the creation of a rapid-rail system from Galveston to Houston to Dallas. The task force felt that, like the Ike Dike, such projects were beyond the scope of their technical expertise and financial authority. The best way to address these questions, they argued, was that "[n]on-deferrable single purpose funding should be appropriated to conduct high-intensity, short duration feasibility studies on a number of projects and policies to determine what solutions are appropriate…to protect and mitigate disaster impacts. World-class experts from government, the private sector and academia should conduct the feasibility studies."[18]

The Aftermath

The task force submitted its response to the Governor's Commission on 10 June 2009, nine months after Ike made landfall. Jemison pushed

---

[17] GHP Disaster Planning and Recovery Task Force, "Recommendations," 5.

[18] Ibid., 5.

forward with the intention of developing further recommendations specific to the Houston area, but her effort was not successful. Task force members drifted away, their most pressing work completed. A survey widely distributed to Houston-area businesses attempting to evaluate the impact of the hurricane and the availability of disaster recovery services received only 42 responses—a great disappointment to Jemison and perhaps an indication that businesses had adjusted and moved on, so that the issue was no longer salient. Turnover at GHP resulted in a loss of support staff assigned to the task force; Jemison ultimately decided to complete a second report to GHP within her own office and, to date, that is where it remains.

Francisco Sanchez and Joni Baird, however, continue to work on the creation of a communication network joining business and government entities when disasters occur. "Public-private partnerships are critical to solving this kind of problem, especially in big cities," says Baird, who had hoped GHP would take on the creation of such a network as an organizational project. "You need a wide perspective, diversity of opinion, and a way to cross boundaries." Sanchez concurs: "You need to have a relationship before the disaster happens. Relationships build trust. You need engagement from all sides from start to finish. It's a circular, self-correcting process: plan, practice, adapt, repeat." The two participate in a work group comprising former task-force members as well as representatives of other large corporations (ExxonMobil and Shell, for instance) and governmental agencies that continued, in 2012, to push to develop a unified communication plan.

And those studies recommended by the Infrastructure group continue to take place. Professor William Merrell of Texas A&M University, Galveston, led a study group to the Netherlands in the summer of 2012 to study the Dutch equivalent of the Ike Dike, although the expensive proposal "has gained little traction in

Houston," according to the *Houston Chronicle*.[19] An alternative set of proposals—smaller projects that could be financed by local bonds—has been advanced by a group of Rice University professors, and the debate continues.[20]

Both Sanchez and Baird feel that, while the task force withered away at the end, it succeeded at its more limited mission, responding to the Governor's Commission. Jemison garnered excellent reviews for her management of the task force process. "Mae Jemison is a masterful facilitator who tried to build consensus," said Joni Baird. "Everyone was heard; no one was diminished. [She] kept us on task and negotiated around disagreements. She is a great problem solver, so I was not surprised." The task force's work also set the stage for continued examination of disaster planning issues. "We have a much better picture of the challenges but we still have a responsibility to find solutions," said Sanchez. And GHP's Jeff Moseley agreed. "A major result of this task force," he said, "is that it has established a process for dialogue, and has given us a template for framing the issues and for working together."

---

[19] Eric Berger, "Ike Dike May Be Among Sandy's Casualties," *Houston Chronicle*, 4 November 2012, http://www.chron.com/news/houston-texas/houston.article/Ike-Dike-may-be-among-Sandy-s-casualties-4005871.php, accessed 9 November 2012.

[20] Ibid.

7

Columbus, Georgia: Rollin' on the River[1]

On 18 September 2013, I found myself sitting at a conference table in a large, windowed room on an upper floor of the Synovus Center in downtown Columbus, Georgia. Around me, enjoying a sumptuous breakfast and talking about the relationship between their businesses and the Columbus community, was a host of Columbus's business elite: Kessel Stelling, president of Synovus and Jimmy Blanchard, the company's former CEO; Jimmy Yancey, former president and CEO of Total Systems (TSYS); Gardiner Garrard, chairman of the board of the Jordan Company, a real estate and private equity investment firm; John Turner from W.C. Bradley Company and Mat Swift, president of W.C. Bradley Real Estate; Mike Gaymon, president of the Greater Columbus Chamber; and Tim Mescon, president of Columbus State University.

The business community of Columbus, particularly over the last thirty years, has had a great tradition of involvement in civic quality-of-life issues, and all of these men uphold that tradition. We were looking out the window at the latest evidence of their success: a whitewater course running through the center of the city. The project itself involved nearly every major civic, business, and governmental organization in the region, and each of these men had had an impact.

---

[1] Thanks to the following Columbus business leaders for speaking with me about the Whitewater project: William B. Turner, John Turner, Mat Swift, Jimmy Blanchard, Jimmy Yancey, Kessel Stelling, Gardiner Garrard, Tim Mescon, Tom Helton and Mike Gaymon. Quotations from these sources are the result of personal interviews conducted in September, October, and November 2013.

But the leadership of the project rested chiefly with one particular urban statesman: John Turner.

Columbus, Georgia, businessman John Turner comes from a family that pretty much defines the concept of "doing good while doing well." The family's W.C. Bradley Company has been a player on the Columbus business scene since its founding in 1885. When his grandfather headed up the company's Bradley-Turner Foundation, says John, "He never considered the money his. He'd support pretty much everything. If you asked for money and came away with nothing, you'd done something wrong." John's father, William B. "Mr. Bill" Turner, is the city's civic philanthropist-in-chief, the strongest voice behind the plans that have steadily revitalized downtown Columbus since the 1980s. Now in his nineties, Mr. Bill is still dreaming up plans to improve his city. It should be no surprise to anyone that other members of the Turner family have stepped up to the civic plate to lead Columbus forward.

John Turner's project may be the most creative of the bunch. He led the complex effort to create the world's longest urban whitewater course on a 2.5-mile stretch of the Chattahoochee River that splits the difference between downtown Columbus and Phenix City, Alabama. Officially labeled the "Chattahoochee River Restoration Project" and locally known as "Whitewater," the effort required an extensive public-private partnership involving two state governments, two cities, the Army Corps of Engineers, the US Fish and Wildlife Service, the Federal Energy Regulatory Commission, and a raft of civic and environmental organizations. The $24.4 million project included the acquisition and demolition of two dams, the development of computer and physical models of the riverbed, and the construction of artificial rapids to enhance the natural rapids already in the river but hidden by the dams. It took fifteen years start to finish.

To place the project in context, you need to understand the relationship between Columbus and its river—in particular, the relationship between the river and the redevelopment of downtown (known as "Uptown") Columbus.

The River at Columbus

The city of Columbus, founded in 1828, sits at the northern-most navigable point on the Chattahoochee River, right where the Cumberland Plateau gives way to the sandy loam and flat elevation of south Georgia. This sudden drop in elevation, which crosses all of central Georgia, is called the Fall Line. Just a bit to the south is what locals call the Gnat Line, in recognition of those pesky biting insects that prefer not to live north of it.

The economy of Columbus was long dominated by the textile industry and the military presence of the US Army's Fort Benning as well as the industries that support it.[2] The site of naval construction facilities, Columbus was the last significant industrial city left standing in the Confederacy and, in April 1865, was the site of the last major battle of the Civil War. Needless to say, the city's industry suffered in the military loss, which occurred a week after the surrender of the Confederate Army at Appomattox, Virginia.[3] From the 1820s, dams on the river provided power to run grist and textile mills in the area. Including the two dams breached for the Whitewater project, six dams impact the river near Columbus, beginning with the Bartlett's Ferry Dam seventeen miles north of the city.

In 1998, when an organization named the Chattahoochee Fall Line Alliance, led by John Turner, began to investigate the possibility of creating a whitewater experience in Columbus, four of those dams—Bartlett's Ferry, Goat Rock, Lake Oliver, and North Highlands—were

---

[2] "History of Columbus, Georgia," http://www.columbusga.org/history, accessed 28 October 2013.

[3] See, for instance, "The Battle of Columbus (Girard, Alabama)," at http://www.exploresouthernhistory.com/battleofcolumbus.html, accessed 3 December 2013.

generating significant hydroelectric power. Two others, located where the river flowed through downtown Columbus, had become less important for power generation because the mills that depended on them for electricity had closed. The City Mills Dam, which crossed the river at Eighteenth Street, was originally a wooden dam built in 1828 to support a corn mill and had been replaced with a stone structure in 1907. It was no longer generating electricity. The Eagle & Phenix Dam, at Front Street near the Dillingham Street Bridge, was built in 1868.[4] Although it was still generating electricity in 1998, by 2002 a fire had destroyed one of its two powerhouses, and its major client, Pillowtex Corporation, had announced that it would close, diminishing the dam's contribution.[5] These last two dams created still-water ponds that covered what had been the Fall Line rapids of the Chattahoochee.

The two in-town dams, while concealing the river's natural whitewater features, created small waterfalls that made for attractive viewing. While there might have been discussion in Columbus about how the river and its features could best be harnessed, John Turner says, "We didn't think we had a river that was broken. It was a beautiful river, and these historic dams created really neat focal points." The same, however, could not be said of the downtown area of Columbus through which the river flowed.

In the 1950s and '60s the mills that had sustained the Columbus economy began to close. Downtown Columbus began a decline typical of many small Southern cities of the era, emptying itself of both people and business. Atlanta urban development consultant and Columbus native Otis White writes:

---

[4] "Chattahoochee River Dams," http://www.brownsguides.com/v/chattahoocheee-river-dams/, accessed 11 November 2013.

[5] Chuck Williams, "Rapid Return—Support Grows for Exposing the Old River and Allowing Rapids to Run Past Downtown," *Columbus* (GA) *Ledger-Enquirer*, 12 May 2002, A-1.

Middle-class housing had long since moved away from downtown. Retail followed in the 1950s, first to shopping centers, later to a regional mall. Entertainment—movie theaters, restaurants, nightclubs—joined the exodus in the 1960s. By the 1970s, many downtown offices had left for new developments near the Interstate highway. A few things remained. City government was downtown, along with some law offices and a lovely community theater, the Springer Opera House. Just south of downtown, there was a historic district, where some of the grand old homes has been rescued and restored. But Broadway, with its vacant storefronts and empty office buildings? Who would drive miles past a mall to shop there? Who would drive past new office parks to work there? As for living downtown, who would be crazy enough to do that?[6]

Most of the business and political leadership of Columbus had given up on downtown; in fact, many could see no reason why downtown might be worth saving. Two of the city's leading business lights, however, thought otherwise: architect Rozier Dedwylder and businessman William B. (Bill) Turner, CEO of the W.C. Bradley Company. The Turner family had been connected with the company since 1917, when D.A. Turner married W.C. Bradley's only daughter, Elizabeth, and began training to manage the company's diversifying assets.[7]

Over the course of its 130-year history, W.C. Bradley Company has operated businesses in "the textiles industry, farm implement manufacturing, row crop and livestock production, wholesale supply businesses meeting the needs of industrial and building contractors, retail businesses in outdoor sports equipment and licensed sports apparel, and barbecue grill manufacturing"[8] as well as real estate development. In 1943, Bradley and Turner also created what later

---

[6] Otis White, *The Great Project* (Apple iBook, 2012) 9.

[7] "A History of Innovation," http:// www.wcbradley.com/history.aspx, accessed 4 November 2013.

[8] "Overview," http://www.wcbradley.com/ovverview.aspx, accessed 4 November 2013.

became the Bradley-Turner Foundation, an entity that has contributed more than \$270 million to charitable, educational, religious, and cultural programs, and community improvements in the Columbus area.[9]

D.A. Turner succeeded W.C. Bradley as the company's chairman of the board upon Bradley's death in 1947. In 1953, D.A. Turner's son Bill was elected president and CEO of the company, rising to the position of vice chairman in 1973, and to chairman in 1982. Presiding over a growing and diversifying company, Bill Turner also wanted his city to grow and prosper—but when he looked out his window, that was not what he saw. [10] (He also did not see the river. Although the W.C. Bradley headquarters building overlooks the Chattahoochee River, it began its life as a cotton warehouse with no windows on the side facing the river. It's little wonder that it took a while to grasp the importance of the river as a "quality of life" asset.)

The Rebirth of Downtown

A mid-1970s attempt at redeveloping downtown, led by Washington, DC, architect Arthur Cotton Moore, was a bust. Moore proposed building a set of leisure-time attractions to bring people back downtown. His ideas included a pedestrian mall, an ice-skating rink, an artists' gallery, and a canal coming off the river. "Downtown was in economic free fall," says Otis White. "There was little political support for doing anything—and certainly not for anything grand— and the canal idea clinched it. In no time, it became known as 'Milton's moat,' after the well-meaning city council member, Milton Hirsch, who had sponsored the planning effort, and quickly sank out of sight, along with the rest of Moore's plans."[11]

Bill Turner and Rozier Dedwylder learned from Hirsch's (and Moore's) mistake. They decide to push for small steps and build on

---

[9] "A History of Innovation."
[10] Ibid.
[11] White, *The Great Project*, 10.

their successes. First they persuaded the city to redevelop a Civil War foundry into a convention and trade center. Then, says Jimmy Blanchard, "We needed a hotel, and eighteen businesses came together and put money into a Hilton right across from the Trade Center. Hotel developers wouldn't do it so we did it ourselves." Their third project turned an old factory into a modern office building.[12] For support, they drew on a strong base of business and civic leaders from several well-known national companies headquartered in Columbus: Synovus, Total Systems (TSYS) and Aflac among them.

In 1983, the formation of an organization called Uptown Columbus, focused on revitalizing downtown by purchasing distressed properties and reselling them to people or groups who would improve them, providing another vehicle for the continued improvement of the city.[13] A Chamber of Commerce-sponsored visit to Chattanooga and the Lupton Foundation in the late 1980s impressed upon Columbus's business and political leaders the need for a vision and strategic planning as the city moved forward.

By the 1990s, the push to redevelop and enhance downtown Columbus was well underway. In 1992, the city opened the first phase of its river walk, now a 22-mile-long riverside walking and biking trail created in response to federal mandated sewer and water upgrades. Mat Swift, president of W.C. Bradley Real Estate, tells the story: "We were going to have to figure out a way to solve this $25 million [combined sewer overflow pipe] problem anyway. I'll never forget it. We were in a meeting and a Water Works guy said, 'We're going to run the pipes down Front Street.' I said, 'No, you're not. I've got real estate all up and down Front Street and I'm not going to have you ruin it. Why don't we consider something else?' I give him credit; he came back and said, 'OK, let's put it along the riverfront and put a river walk on top of it.'" The infrastructure for one of Columbus's

---

[12] Ibid., 11.
[13] Chuck Williams, "Defining Uptown," *Columbus* (GA) *Ledger-Enquirer,* 29 April 2001, A-1.

biggest attractions was combined with and financed by sewer construction.

The river walk was transformative. Otis White reports, "From the moment the first stretch was opened, the river walk was a hit, drawing Columbus residents back to the river and reintroducing them to the downtown. In addition, with its graceful brick paths, resting areas, and inspiring views of the Chattahoochee, the river walk convinced many that Columbus could accomplish big projects with style."[14] Bill Turner, by this time retired as chairman of W.C. Bradley Company, observed, "[The Riverwalk] is a place everybody feels they have a piece of. When the Riverwalk was built, everybody saw the possibilities. Every great city has a place where there is a sense of ownership. The river and Riverwalk are ours."[15]

Other business-sponsored projects followed in short order. A new softball complex captured the 1996 Olympics women's softball competition. A new civic center was built. Credit card processer Total Systems built a large new campus downtown. A new performing arts center brought not only outstanding productions but also the School of Music at Columbus State University, along with its theater and art programs, to downtown—and that meant a need for new residential space, restaurants, and shopping for new downtown residents. The $22.5 million Synovus Center rose over the river just below the falls created by the Eagle & Phenix Dam.[16] Columbus barely recognized this new downtown.

A New Vision for the River

Into this atmosphere of resurgence stepped John Turner with his new vision for the river, looking to make one more contribution to the downtown renaissance. His idea was not original, he says. Turner

---

[14] White, *The Great Project*, 13.

[15] Quoted in Chuck Williams, "Flowing to the Gathering at the River," *Columbus* (GA) *Ledger-Enquirer*, 7 September 2003, A-1.

[16] Ibid.

traces the idea of an urban whitewater course back to Neal Wickham, who owned an outdoor equipment company in Columbus in the 1970s. Wickham and one of his employees, Joseph Smith (who had spent time kayaking and guiding river trips on the Ocoee River in Tennessee, later the site of the 1996 Olympic whitewater course, and other Georgia and North Carolina rivers) "just kind of started talking about wouldn't it be neat if we could remove these dams and expose these rapids, because [it] was a historical fact that they used to exist," says Turner. "There were some old photographs and a landscape in the Columbus museum [depicting] the river prior to the dams being here, so it was known that there were rapids."

Wickham remembers being more proactive. He told the *Columbus Ledger-Enquirer* that, "he walked both banks of the river with a video camera and prepared a presentation that he gave to W.C. Bradley chairman Bill Turner in the early 1990s. Not long afterward, Turner's son John Turner took hold of the project...."[17]

Turner's interest was more civic than sport-related, however: "None of us [in the early discussions] were avid paddlers. This wasn't the skateboarders who wanted a skateboard park. These were folks who were looking at this strictly from the standpoint of how unique it could be for a community. Imagine! How cool would that be, in the middle of town! Even then communities were starting to understand that maybe things like water and sewer and industrial sites weren't the assets of the future." Turner had a vision of a "really cool community" with a special quality of life, and he saw a new use of river as the path to his goal.

Turner's first step was to legitimize his effort. Through Uptown Columbus, on whose board he served, he pulled together an ad hoc committee titled the Chattahoochee Fall Line Alliance. The loosely

---

[17] Mike Owen, "River Guides See Whitewater Project Becoming a Major Regional Attraction," *Columbus* (GA) *Ledger-Enquirer*, 25 August 2012, http://infoweb.newsbank.com.afpls.idm.oclc.org/iw-search/we/InfoWeb, accessed 1 May 2013.

structured and somewhat fluid group included representatives from the Columbus and Phenix City, Alabama, governments, the Lower Chattahoochee Riverkeeper, the Greater Columbus and Phenix City-Russell County chambers of commerce, the Historic Columbus Foundation, the Alabama Rivers Alliance, the US Fish and Wildlife Service, and Georgia Power Company. [18] The committee made information gathering its first task: What kind of whitewater activity might be possible?

Early thinking centered on constructing a special whitewater channel bypassing one or both of the in-town dams, using the drop produced by the dam to create artificial rapids. The channel seemed a good place to start, thought Turner. "The thinking was," he says, "these are historic dams and we don't own them, and one of them is generating some electricity and so the notion of removing these dams seemed to be just sort of a crazy idea." A small gift from the Bradley Turner Foundation allowed Turner and his committee to bring in as consultants John Anderson and Rick McLaughlin, designers of the Ocoee River whitewater course that had hosted the 1996 Olympics.

Anderson and McLaughlin looked at the concept of a bypass channel at multiple locations and in proximity to both of the dams. Turner remembers: "What they told us was, 'you can do this and we've certainly done this in other places but it's incredibly expensive and we can't recreate the river you already have. You have big rapids and we normally do this sort of thing in places that don't have them. We are creating artificial rapids where we're using a dam and the drop of the dam to distribute these rapids through a bypass channel.' They also said these dams [City Mills and Eagle & Phoenix], had really outlived their useful lives. They were in disrepair, and one of them was generating no electricity at the time. That sort of started the conversation" about breaching the dams and using the original riverbed as the whitewater course.

---

[18] Williams "Rapid Return," A-1.

Anderson told the *Columbus Ledger-Enquirer*: "At the time, we were charged with looking at some sort of whitewater course. It was a head-scratcher. The more I looked, the thing I found most attractive was below each dam—especially the Eagle & Phenix."[19] Then, he said, it hit him: "The whitewater course was the river itself. Let the river do the work." The *Ledger-Enquirer* summarized the results of Anderson's study this way: "...if the two dams—one at the Eagle & Phenix Mill and the other at City Mills—were breached or removed, a free-flowing river would create rapids suitable for recreational rafting, kayaking and fishing." [20] Turner recalls, "They looked at our river and said, 'The Olympics should have been here.' It wasn't that the Ocoee's not a great river because it absolutely is, but what they recognized was that this is a great river at a place that has parking and hotel rooms and restaurants and bathrooms."

In addition to Anderson's recommendations, Turner received a visit from Glen Coffee of the Army Corps of Engineers, who had been included in the Alliance's early discussions. Out of the blue, says Turner, Coffee called to say the project might be of interest to the Corps of Engineers, which had access to funds for projects to "restore or repair aquatic resources that have been damaged by man or nature."[21] The Corps's focus was environmental, not recreational, but senior planner Glenn Coffee, who conducted a study in response to Anderson's findings, concluded that the project had merit from an environmental standpoint as well, and recommended a further feasibility study at a cost of $400,000, paid for by the Corps and requiring about a year to complete. The Corps also required a local government sponsor to undertake a study,[22] so Turner presented the proposal to the Columbus Council, asking that they endorse the

---

[19] Ibid.

[20] Chuck Williams, "Changes to Dams Sought—Moves Could Create Rapids in Downtown Columbus for Rafting," *Columbus* (GA) *Ledger-Enquirer*, 15 May 2002, C-1.

[21] Williams, "Rapid Return," A-1.

[22] Ibid.

Corps study and emphasizing that, "we are not asking for any kind of commitment, other than for them to commit that they are interested." All costs would be borne by the Corps, and a favorable recommendation from the Corps could qualify the project for federal matching grants.[23] On 21 May 2002, the council agreed to sponsor the study.[24]

A Long, Slow Process

As it turned out, "about a year" was an incredible understatement— and only referred to the beginning phase of a very long process. The feasibility study, conducted by the Corps's Mobile District office and completed in September 2004, recommended partially removing the two dams—but that was only the first in a series of hurdles. The Atlanta Regional Office approved the district recommendations in May 2005, and the project was then placed on a national list of approved projects.[25] Turner and the Fall Line Alliance planned to use Corps funding to support research and design activities, but that funding, subject to the federal appropriations process, was year-to-year and not always certain. "It happened in fits and starts," he reflects. "And the contracting for some of the professional work [to which] federal guidelines applied was just incredibly slow."

Additionally, for the Corps of Engineers, other priorities intervened. Speaking with the *Ledger-Enquirer* when the House Appropriations Committee approved a $2 million allocation for the project in the fiscal 2007 federal budget, Turner acknowledged, "[Project approval] has been slow but it has always been on track. We

---

[23] Williams, "Changes to Dams Sought," C-1.

[24] Chuck Williams, "City Supports River Study—May Remove Dams for Kayaking, Rafting and Fishing," *Columbus* (GA) *Ledger-Enquirer*, 22 May 2002, C-8.

[25] See Erin Simpson, "The Columbus Connection—Two Cities Working Together More," *Columbus* (GA) *Ledger-Enquirer*, 26 February 2005, L-1, and Chuck Williams, "River Plan Clears Committee—Westmoreland Pushes for Whitewater Funding," *Columbus* (GA) *Ledger-Enquirer*, 23 June 2005, L-1.

have been working quietly with the Corps of Engineers on the investigation of the project. Hurricane Katrina and Iraq have slowed the process dramatically. The Corps of Engineers, obviously, has been focused on other things."[26]

In fact, the long approval process required by Corps of Engineers protocol gave the Columbus contingent valuable time to refine and evaluate their vision. John Turner in particular had all along regarded their efforts as "a conversation, not a sales pitch." As funding from the Corps dribbled in, the Alliance used the federal dollars to move the research and planning forward. This option made sense for a project to which they were not yet ready to commit. Says Turner, "We didn't want to go out and go public with something we weren't even sure about. We didn't want to go raise a lot of private money for studies and then say, 'Uh oh, this is probably not going to work. We can't do this.' So we had the federal funding and that's what we used to get us to the point where we were willing to make a commitment." Several daunting issues faced the Alliance; how they were resolved would determine whether the project went forward.

First, the dams that would have to be breeched did not belong to the people who wanted the breech them. The City Mills Dam, which was no longer producing power, was owned by City Mills, Inc., whose president Charles D. Bower, was a local businessman who had expressed support for the whitewater project. The Eagle & Phenix Dam, which was still active when project planning began, was owned by CHI Energy of Stamford, Connecticut. By May 2002, however, one of the dam's two powerhouses had been damaged by fire, dramatically reducing its production capacity, and the dam's major customer, Pillowtex Corporation, had announced its imminent closure.[27]

---

[26] Chuck Williams, "Funding Lifts Hopes of Whitewater Fans—House Committee Slates $2 Million for Chattahoochee Construction Work," *Columbus* (GA) *Ledger-Enquirer*, 18 May 2006, C-1.

[27] Williams, "Rapid Return," A-1.

Into this scenario stepped Mat Swift, president of the W.C. Bradley Company Real Estate Division, acting on behalf of Uptown Columbus. Recognizing the long-term strategic value of both dams to the overall development of the riverfront, in September 2003 he negotiated the purchase of the Eagle & Phenix Dam and an option on the City Mills Dam, whose purchase was finalized later. [28] (Still later, Swift would also purchase the Eagle & Phenix Mills for redevelopment as loft condominiums.) The Alliance decided to move forward with the Eagle & Phenix Dam purchase in spite of the fact that the whitewater project was not yet a "go." Turner explained to the *Ledger-Enquirer*: "The reason we felt it was safe to acquire the dam not knowing the results of the study is because the dam and its property are critical to the entire Eagle & Phenix [redevelopment] project. It is bigger than just the whitewater. The dam is needed for both projects."[29] Ownership for the dam transferred to Uptown Columbus until the project could move forward.

Funding for the purchase came from a "significant early gift" of $2 million from the Bradley-Turner Foundation. $1.25 million of that gift was used to purchase the Eagle & Phenix Dam; the balance, combined with a later $500 million appropriation from Phenix City[30] and a grant from the Trust for Public Lands, provided the funds for the purchase of the City Mills Dam after the decision to move forward with the project. Phenix City had a particular interest in the City Mills purchase. "Along with the dam," says Turner, "we were acquiring 1.4 miles of river frontage on the Alabama side of the river." He told the *Ledger-Enquirer*: "It would allow us to largely protect 2.5 miles of the riverbank on both sides if we make the acquisition."

---

[28] Chuck Williams, "Purchase of Dam Puts Whitewater Closer to Reality—Uptown Columbus Buys Property for $1.23 Million," *Columbus* (GA) *Ledger-Enquirer*, 24 September 2003, A-1.

[29] Ibid.

[30] Ibid.

Purchasing the Eagle & Phenix Dam and optioning City Mills solved one of the Alliance's big problems. They also needed to deal with the historic preservation interests in Columbus. This proved an easier nut to crack. While the dams and their powerhouses were considered historic structures that illustrated Columbus's mill past, the river in its original configuration was considered historic as well. The Historic Columbus Foundation voted to support the river restoration project, but wanted the dams breached rather than destroyed, and the powerhouses and other structures preserved as much as was possible. Turner agreed. He told the newspaper, "Our thinking is to leave as much of the dam abutments as possible to retain a historic perspective. What we would be exposing is a historic riverbed."[31]

In fact, public support for the project was high in the early days, and grew from there. By May 2002, the river restoration had been endorsed by the boards of Uptown Columbus, the Greater Columbus Chamber of Commerce, and the Chattahoochee Riverkeeper, as well as by the Historic Columbus Foundation. By the time the whitewater course opened, eighteen agencies—federal, state, local, environmental, historic presentation, and recreation—were part of the partnership. "What other project puts the Sierra Club and the developer on the same team?" asks Mat Swift. "I haven't seen that ever. But it touched them all, because it was restoring the river. It was economic development, it was environmental, it was recreation, it was historic, and so [support] just built."

With the dams purchased and the public on his side, Turner still faced two big questions. The first: What would the new river look like? "We want to make sure it delivers on the promise of a more beautiful river," Turner said. What he and the Alliance were proposing, he realized, would change the character of the river dramatically. Now there were two spillways with flat water behind them. The change he was proposing would replace two dams with

---

[31] Williams, "Rapid Return," A-1.

ponds behind them with two-miles-worth of fast-moving, noisy whitewater.[32]

The attempt to answer this question required a number of sophisticated studies of the river. During the time required by the Corps of Engineers for their approval process, and aided by a series of federal appropriations for the project, the Alliance "compiled river surveys, sonar readings, computer models and aerial photos, gaining a much clearer assessment of what they can do and how much it will cost," said the *Ledger-Enquirer*.[33] Uptown Columbus, in submitting the whitewater project for a Georgia Planning Association award, emphasized that during the more than ten years that the project had been under consideration, they had used the most sophisticated technology and "probed [the river], sonared it, computer-modeled it, photographed it, biologically sampled it, historic-resource surveyed it, and master planned it. The benefit of all that work is that we now know the river very well and fully appreciate the dramatic impact that restoring it will have on this community."[34] While all of these studies indicated that removing the dams would reveal promised whitewater rapids, the tests still did not provide absolute certainty in the minds of those making the decisions.

Meanwhile, whitewater experts and engineers John Anderson and Rick McLaughlin were tasked with designing a course that would be both safe and attractive at the varying levels of water flow and

---

[32] Ibid.

[33] Tim Chitwood, "Columbus Plans to Have Whitewater Course Ready in 2012—Officials Say Breaching Dams Could Create 'Monster Waves' and Major Economic Impact," *Columbus* (GA) *Ledger-Enquirer*, 27 April 2010, http://infoweb.newsbank.com.afpls.idm.oclc.org/iw-search/we/InfoWeb, accessed 1 May 2013.

[34] Uptown Columbus, "The Chattahoochee River Restoration Project: Submission for the 2010 Georgia Planning Association Chapter Awards—Outstanding Initiative" (Fall 2010), http://www.phenixcityal.us/edo/Sites/Phenix_City/Documents/Economic%20Development/Chattahoochee%20River%20Restoration%20Project.pdf, accessed 19 November 2013, 4.

volume that would result from upstream generation of hydroelectric power. (The range of flow was from 800 to 13,000 cubic feet per second, with the water level fluctuating 5 to 7 feet.)[35] At their request, in 2010 Alden Labs of Holden, Massachusetts, constructed a physical model of the riverbed, about the size of an elementary school gymnasium, to demonstrate what the riverbed would look like without water, how the river would flow and where the rapids would build up. In November 2010, after the project had been formally announced and fund-raising had begun, the committee traveled to Massachusetts to view the $300,000 model. Turner felt this was a necessary step. "Those computers can't accurately duplicate what can happen with a free-flowing river," he told the *Ledger-Enquirer*.[36] But even the model didn't eliminate his anxiety. "We had these computer models and these physical models and all this whiz-bang stuff we'd done to try and understand it, but we didn't know for sure" until the dams were breached, he said later.

Calculating the Cost

A final set of questions centered on cost: Would the project be worth the expense—and would Turner and his committee be able to raise the money to fund it? Early estimates put the cost of the project the $6- to $7-million-dollar range, with up to $5 million dollars available as a grant from the Corps of Engineers with a 35 percent local match required. [37] By 2006, the cost estimate was $13 million.[38] In 2007,

---

[35] Ibid.

[36] Sara Pauff, "River Restoration Committee Gets a Look at Model of Whitewater Course," *Columbus* (GA) *Ledger-Enquirer*, 24 November 2010, http://infoweb.newsbank.com.afpls.idm.oclc.org/iw-search/we/InfoWeb, accessed 1 May 2013.

[37] Chuck Williams, "Chattahoochee River Restoration Project—Rapid Return Removal of Dams Would Bring Whitewater back to Chattahoochee," *Columbus* (GA) *Ledger-Enquirer*, 25 March 2003, C-1.

following an extensive study of the river, Army Corps of Engineers' contractor CH2M Hill was hired to produce a plan for how to do the work while maintaining the minimum water flow required on the river, as well as a more solid cost estimate.[39] The new number was larger yet; when the project was formally announced in April 2010, the cost was pegged at $23 million.

The change in numbers came from a more complete understanding of what the project entailed. Breaching the dams, it became clear, would not be a simple process. Both dams were in fact a complex, with newer stone or masonry dams built downstream from older wooden structures, all of them in poor condition. Excavation of the riverbed to aid fish migration and construction of a weir at the North Highland Dam to compensate for a change in water level when the pond behind the City Mills Dam disappeared were also needed.[40]

A study by Columbus State University, though, indicated that the cost of the project was far outweighed by its economic benefits. Uptown Columbus president Richard Bishop announced the study's projections: 700 new jobs; 188,000 visitors a year (144,000 of those from out of town); $300,000 a year from increased hotel/motel taxes; and $1.7 million in sales tax, for an annual economic impact of $42 million.[41] These numbers were fueled by the unique nature of the Columbus venue. Other Southeastern whitewater facilities—the Ocoee River in southeastern Tennessee and the Nantahala in western

---

[38] Chuck Williams, "Funding Lifts Hopes of Whitewater Fans—House Committee Slates $2 Million for Chattahoochee Construction Work," *Columbus* (GA) *Ledger-Enquirer*, 18 May 2006, C-1.

[39] Tim Chitwood, "Down to the Fall Line," *Columbus* (GA) *Ledger-Enquirer*, 29 July 2007, C-1.

[40] Ibid.

[41] Tim Chitwood, "Update: Proponents Say Columbus' $23 Million Chattahoochee River Whitewater Project's Read to Launch," *Columbus* (GA) *Ledger-Enquirer*, 26 April 2010, http://infoweb.newsbank.com.afpls.idm. oclc.org/iw-search/we/InfoWeb, accessed 1 May 2013.

North Carolina—were in rural areas with limited access to hotels, restaurants, and other tourist comforts. But, as downtown merchant Brent Troncalli told the *Ledger-Enquirer*, "Columbus is the only river I'm aware of where you can come in the morning, go down the river, then go to lunch at multiple restaurants, go to a bar, go shopping if you want to, and then you can go back in the afternoon and go rafting again if you want. You can also go to the Riverwalk. There's so many things that are so close by each other. That's really what's going to make this different."[42]

So the results, Turner and his associates concluded, would likely justify the expense. Now, how to raise the money? Here the Columbus business community was critical. Turner's strategy was to obtain several major gifts, and leverage those to appeal for the rest. He says, "There were four big commitments that we went and got first: the city of Columbus, the W.C. Bradley Company, Total Systems (TSYS), and Aflac—and once we made those four calls and got those four commitments then we said, 'OK, we feel like this is achievable.'" The city of Columbus committed $5 million over three years; W.C. Bradley made a $5 million donation; TSYS and Aflac (through the Aflac Foundation) contributed "in the million dollar range."

Turner emphasizes that the decision to go forward with the project was not made until all of these issues—dam procurement, historic foundation and public support, the appearance of the reengineered river, and the achievement of a base level of financing—had been addressed to the satisfaction of an "inner circle" of decision-makers connected to Uptown Columbus, which controlled the dam properties and took responsibility for completing and operating the project. That group, with some additions, formed the committee that

---

[42] Tony Adams, "Whitewater Rafting Course to Make Big Splash on Columbus Area Economy—City Savoring Economic Potential for Whitewater Course on Chattahoochee River in Downtown Area," *Columbus* (GA) *Ledger-Enquirer*, 25 September 2011, http://infoweb.newsbank.com.afpls.idm.oclc.org/iw-search/we/InfoWeb, accessed 1 May 2013.

would be directly responsible for implementing the project, now called the Chattahoochee River Restoration Project. This group, an official committee operating under the control of the board of directors of Uptown Columbus, included, in addition to John Turner, W.C. Bradley Company CEO Steve Butler, W.C. Bradley Real Estate president Mat Swift, former city manager Carmen Cavezza, architect Ed Burdeshaw, deputy city manager David Arrington, Greater Columbus Chamber of Commerce president Mike Gaymon, and Uptown Columbus president Richard Bishop. Retired Columbus Water Works director Billy Turner (no relation to John) served as project director.[43]

It's a Go!

It was now time to get the show on the road. On 26 April 2010, John Turner, Richard Bishop, and project engineer John Anderson stood on the Fourteenth Street Bridge in downtown Columbus and announced plans to build a downtown whitewater course by 2012 and a fund-raising campaign to finance the project under the logo "Ready2Raft." Turner described a course that would cover 2.5 miles with a 40-foot drop in elevation over the length of the run. The plan, he said, was to divert the river and use heavy equipment in the river bed to take apart the Eagle & Phenix and City Mills dams, and then construct an engineered whitewater course that fit the river's more natural flow. "We've been dealt an incredible hand here," he said. He expected construction to begin in May 2011. Columbus had the opportunity to "restore what a big Fall Line river used to be." Anderson declared that after breaching the Eagle & Phenix Dam, at full flow the Chattahoochee would present "a world-class whitewater run." Bishop offered the results of Columbus State University's economic analysis and concluded, "This is serious economic development."[44]

---

[43] Uptown Columbus, "The Chattahoochee River Restoration Project," 2.

[44] Chitwood, "Columbus Plans to Have Whitewater Course Ready in 2012," 27 April 2010.

Two tasks immediately presented themselves: decommissioning the dams and obtaining the final permits, and raising the rest of the money required for construction. Finding the money proved the easier of the two tasks. $10 million of the money already in place was public funding—$5 million from the city of Columbus, and $5 million from the Corps of Engineers. $500 million came from Phenix City, Alabama; another $600,000 grant from the National Oceanic and Atmospheric Administration completed the "public money" segment of the financing. The majority of the donations, $13.8 million, came from private contributions—ranging from the $5 million W.C. Bradley gift to contributions of a few thousand dollars from individuals. Turner, who says his major contribution during this phase of the effort was fund-raising, reported that "private money" gifts to the project included more than fifty major donors (chief among them the Bradley-Turner Foundation, TSYS, and Aflac and its foundation), including around $1.7 million from donors outside of Columbus who had a particular interest in the environmental focus of the project.[45]

The fund-raising argument—particularly the pitch directed at the local business community—went beyond a push to improve the river for environmental reasons, though. At the core, says Turner, was an impulse to make Columbus a place that was attractive to young people. Columbus had long had an image as a sleepy Southern town—not at all a place of action. That quality of life issue was important to the future of Columbus; if its industries, now more finance and technology-oriented than manufacturing, were to grow, young, technology-literate employees would need to be recruited, and would have to be willing to move to Columbus. Turner says, "Take, for example, TSYS. TSYS has historically had a challenge in

---

[45] Tony Adams, "$24.4 Million Chattahoochee River Restoration Project a Blend of Public, Private Funding," *Columbus* (GA) *Ledger-Enquirer*, 6 April 2013, http://infoweb.newsbank.com.afpls.idm.oclc.org/iw-search/we/Info-Web, accessed 1 May 2013.

recruiting brainpower that they need in Columbus, Georgia. That requires the right bait, So the message to them was that if we could become a truly cool small town along the lines of an Austin, a Greenville, a Charleston, a Boulder, then it's not going to be such a daunting task to convince folks that they should live here." The changes wrought by the new Columbus State University downtown campus reinforced the argument: creative young people had awakened the downtown area, and they could do the same for the city's most important business enterprises.

Coupled with the popularity the whitewater project had developed over the twelve years it had been under discussion, the "quality of life" argument made for incredibly effective fund-raising. Mat Swift, who was also a major moneyman for the project, observed, "I can count on one hand the people that turned us down. Out of all the fund-raising deals that I've done, that is not the normal case. Normally, you're lucky if you get a 50 percent conversion back on your calls. The amazing thing is this project transcended the tough times. People were so excited about it that they were willing to make some commitments."[46]

Permits were harder to come by. The project required three major sets of permissions. The Federal Energy Regulatory Commission (FERC) had to decommission the dams—withdraw their authority to generate power—so that the dams could be breached. The Army Corps of Engineers needed to authorize the removal of dredged or excavated material from the river.[47] Finally, the Alabama and Georgia state governments needed to permit possible access points

---

[46] Ibid.

[47] Tim Chitwood, "Olympian Whitewater Competitors Support Plan to Roll out Course—Contractors Chosen, City Needs Permits to Start Course with Potential to be Whitewater Destination," *Columbus* (GA) *Ledger-Enquirer*, 25 February 2011, http://infoweb.newsbank.com.afpls.idm.oclc.org/iw-search/we/InfoWeb, accessed 1 May 2013.

on the river so that contractors could get to the riverbed to work.[48] Those contractors, identified in February 2011 by Richard Bishop, were Batson-Cook Construction, Alexander Contracting, and Scott Bridge Company.[49]

Project director Billy Turner hoped to obtain the permits in time to begin work during the summer of 2011, but the effort took longer than expected, even with the Corps of Engineers supporting the project. "Permitting to do anything in the river is typically your worst nightmare," said John Turner in a May 2013 interview. "We had the Corps of Engineers on our team, so [that] made it a bad dream and not a nightmare."[50] Finally, in August 2011, work began, and on September 22, the official ceremonial groundbreaking—labeled "Riverblasting"—for the project occurred.[51] Mayor Teresa Tomlinson noted the importance of the occasion: "What we do here today is as critical to the history of Columbus as when the first stone was laid for the first mill on these shores of this great river. This is going to change this city and take us into that next era just as sure as that first mill did."[52]

---

[48] Kirsten J. Barnes, "Whitewater Group Seeks Permits in Alabama for $23 Project," *Columbus* (GA) *Ledger-Enquirer*, 9 December 2010, http://infoweb.newsbank.com.afpls.idm.oclc.org/iw-search/we/InfoWeb, accessed 1 May 2013.

[49] Chitwood, "Olympian Whitewater Competitors Support Plan to Roll out Course," 25 February 2011.

[50] Tomy Adams, "Whitewater Project's Top Proponent Reflects on Long Journey to Get Chattahoochee Park Open," *Columbus* (GA) *Ledger-Enquirer*, 20 May 2013, http://infoweb.newsbank.com.afpls.idm.oclc.org/iw-search/we/InfoWeb, accessed 20 November 2013.

[51] Mike Owen, "Whitewater Rafting Project: Hundreds Come Out for 'Riverblasting'—Crowd Gathers for Ceremonial Start to Whitewater Project," *Columbus* (GA) *Ledger-Enquirer*, 23 September 2011, http://infoweb.newsbank.com.afpls.idm.oclc.org/iw-search/we/InfoWeb, accessed 1 May 2013.

[52] Ibid.

For the next year and a half, while some behind-the-scenes fundraising continued, the River Restoration Project was mainly in the hands of the contractors. By the date of "Riverblasting," reported the *Ledger-Enquirer*, "workers with Batson-Cook, the construction company that is handling the project, have built a 'haul road' on the west bank near 13th Street down into the river just below the Eagle & Phenix Dam.... Work had begun there to prepare two sets of rapids before the Eagle & Phenix Dam will be gradually breached."[53] Reporter Chuck Williams watched the construction from a distance until mid-February 2012, when he ventured down to the riverbed, then wrote:

> They are building the ultimate amusement park ride. That signature rapid at the Eagle & Phenix will rival any rapid you can ride in North Georgia or the hills of southern Tennessee. The course is being built in and around the large rocks that make up the historic Fall Line.... Tons of concrete have been poured into the Chattahoochee at the Eagle & Phenix Dam. Concrete-filled bags have been strategically placed along the river bottom to make this course safer and take away some of the places a rafter or kayaker could get trapped under water. None of this should be visible when the project is completed....[54]

This construction progress set up the next big event: blasting a hole in the Eagle & Phenix Dam.

Breaching the Eagle & Phenix Dam actually required two explosions. The first, on March 14, opened a fifty-foot hole in the stone and masonry structure on the Alabama side of the river. The size of the blast disappointed some of the more than one thousand onlookers (all in carefully controlled locations), one of whom was

---

[53] Ibid.

[54] Chuck Williams, "Everything Flows and Nothing Stays," *Columbus (GA) Ledger-Enquirer*, 21 February 2012, http://infoweb.newsbank.com.afpls.idm.oclc.org/iw-search/we/InfoWeb, accessed 1 May 2013.

heard to remark "I've seen car crashes bigger than that."[55] The second blast, four days later and playing to a much smaller crowd, was more impressive, sending water and debris more than four stories into the air and blowing away an additional seventy-five feet of dam. For John Turner, the blasts were one of the more nerve-wracking parts of the project. "I can't tell you how much anxiety there was," he says. "We were so terrified about what would happen when we saw this river for the first time, because there was no turning back. We weren't going to rebuild the dam. So we blew the dam and we finally got to a point where we could start to see the river and there was a big rapid supposed to appear just below the Fourteenth Street Bridge—and it was there. A big rapid was supposed to appear upstream just north of the TSYS campus—and it was there. It was a tremendous relief."

The contractors went back to work, removing debris and sculpting the rapids below the remains of the Eagle & Phenix Dam and excavating a fish habitat channel between Eagle & Phenix and City Mills.[56] In October, Uptown Columbus CEO Richard Bishop announced that his organization had entered into a memorandum of understanding with both the city of Columbus and Phenix City to manage the whitewater park;[57] by December, Uptown had named two outfitters—Whitewater Express of Atlanta and Nantahala

---

[55] Tim Chitwood, "Update: One Section of Eagle & Phenix Dam is Breached with Blast, Another goes Sunday—Some Observers Expected a Bigger Bang," *Columbus* (GA) *Ledger-Enquirer*, 20 March 2012, http://infoweb.newsbank.com.afpls.idm.oclc.org/iw-search/we/InfoWeb, accessed 1 May 2013.

[56] Tim Chitwood, "Whitewater Project: Outfitter Praises Columbus' New Wave, Prospects," *Columbus* (GA) *Ledger-Enquirer*, 30 March 2012, http://infoweb.newsbank.com.afpls.idm.oclc.org/iw-search/we/InfoWeb, accessed 1 May 2013.

[57] Mike Owen, "Whitewater Project Will Use Separate Outfitters for 2 Sides," *Columbus* (GA) *Ledger-Enquirer*, 3 October 2012, http://infoweb.newsbank.com.afpls.idm.oclc.org/iw-search/we/InfoWeb, accessed 20 November 2013.

Outdoor Center of Bryson City, North Carolina—to run the whitewater trips.[58] (Nantahala Outdoor Center would pull out before the course opened.)[59]

By January 2013, the City Mills Dam had also been breached in two places, and Georgia Power Company was preparing to construct a weir, a raised portion of riverbed, to back water against the base of the up-river North Highland Dam so its turbines could work properly. The put-in for rafters was to be just below the weir. On Thursday, January 31, the Uptown Columbus committee unveiled its signature piece of technology, a $400,000 wave-shaper installed on the Georgia side of the river just below the Old Eagle & Phenix powerhouse. The device is designed to control the shape of the rapid across various levels of water flow.[60]

While elements of the course were not yet complete (some roads remained unfinished, parts of the City Mills Dam had not yet been removed, and the permanent put-in on the Georgia side of the river was not yet built), Uptown Columbus and its committee were ready to make an announcement: the whitewater course would open on 25 May 2013. Speaking from the newly renovated Fourteenth Street bridge with leaders—business, civic, and political—from both Columbus and Phenix City watching, reported the *Ledger-Enquirer*,

---

[58] Tim Chitwood, "Outfitter Expects Whitewater Trips Here to Start June 1—Whitewater Express, Nantahala Outdoor Center to Run Local Course," *Columbus* (GA) *Ledger-Enquirer*, 13 December 2012, http://infoweb.newsbank.com.afpls.idm.oclc.org/iw-search/we/InfoWeb, accessed 20 November 2013.

[59] Chuck Williams, "Update: Remaining Outfitter Reduces Rates as Other Company Pulls Out of Chattahoochee Whitewater Course," *Columbus* (GA) *Ledger-Enquirer*, 8 May 2013, http://infoweb.newsbank.com.afpls.idm.oclc.org/iw-search/we/InfoWeb, accessed 20 November 2013.

[60] Tim Chitwood, "Whitewater Wave Machine Cranks Up as Project Proceeds," *Columbus* (GA) *Ledger-Enquirer*, 31 January 2013, http://infoweb.newsbank.com.afpls.idm.oclc.org/iw-search/we/InfoWeb, accessed 1 May 2013.

"W.C. Bradley Co. executive John Turner, the vision and push behind the 12-year project, sounded more like a preacher than anything else. And he was preaching to the choir. 'Isn't this one of the coolest places in the world?' Turner asked as he stood with his back to the course's signature spot a couple of blocks down the river. 'Can I get an amen?' He did."[61]

Opening Day

Saturday, May 25, was a big day for Columbus, Georgia. John Turner recalls: "Opening day our hope was that folks would show up to see this new river. We weren't sure [they would come]. We were having a kind of a groundbreaking and there's this island looking at the Georgia channel. This entire island was full; it was standing room only. There was a long [railing] up above where the Eagle & Phenix powerhouses are, where it was three-deep on the railing looking down on the site. All the bridges were packed with people. It was just an incredible setting and when we walked out there that morning it was like, 'Wow! Folks did show up.'"

The 10 a.m. ceremony included speeches by mayors, environmentalists, and businessmen, giving credit to the many folks who had contributed to making the whitewater project happen, supplemented by trumpets and cannon volleys. But the "one star of this great, big story," observed John Turner, standing in front of a rapid named Heaven's Gate, "is this river." Whitewater Express rafts carried at least 460 customers down the river between 11 a.m. and sunset. (Owner Dan Gilbert had projected 300.) Rafters were excited about their trips, dubbing the rapids "legit" and "excellent" and wishing the trip had lasted longer. Further down the river in calmer water, dragon boat races provided entertainment for more onlookers. One

---

[61] Chuck Williams, "Chattahoochee River Whitewater Course to Open Memorial Day Weekend," *Columbus* (GA) *Ledger-Enquirer*, 7 March 2013, http://infoweb.newsbank.com.afpls.idm.oclc.org/iw-search/we/InfoWeb, accessed 24 June 2013.

restaurant opened at 10:45 to handle the "lunchtime rush"—which lasted until 4:30 p.m. [62]

"After the ceremony," Turner reported, "I'm walking to my car in Uptown and this person from out of town who had driven here to look at this river, to see the river, said, 'Where do y'all park around here?' If you live in Columbus that is music to your ears. We have never had a parking problem in downtown Columbus, but we do now. Every merchant in Uptown that weekend broke a record. Uptown Columbus business improvement district—they do the clean up and everything—they couldn't keep up with the garbage on the streets from the restaurants. They just couldn't keep up with the activity. We had [hundreds] of people in the river and we had many times that number all along the banks of the river, and it's still happening today."

The Columbus media and the business community have been emphatic in crediting Turner with the success of the whitewater project. "John Turner owned this project," said Uptown Columbus president Richard Bishop at the opening day ceremonies. "He was our general manager, our coach, and our quarterback. He kept this project on track for 12-plus years."[63] Turner is quick to give credit to others—his wife, Georgia Power Company, and the Army Corps of Engineers in particular—and says, "There's nothing singular or individual about it."[64] That is true—it is not possible to give credit to only one person when speaking of a project which includes two city governments, two state governments, the federal government,

---

[62] Chuck Williams, "Chattahoochee Whitewater Opens with Grand Ceremony;" Chuck Williams, "Rafters Proclaim Course 'Excellent,' Rapids 'Legit;'" and Sonya Sorich, "River Festivities Change Downtown's Perception," *Columbus* (GA) *Ledger-Enquirer*, 25 May 2013, http://infoweb.newsbank.com.afpls.idm.oclc.org/iw-search/we/InfoWeb, accessed 24 June 2013.

[63] Williams, "Chattahoochee Whitewater Opens with Grand Ceremony," 25 May 2013.

[64] Ibid.

innumerable government agencies connected to all of those entities, an active and tight-knit business community, and dozens of private organizations as well. It is fair to say, though, that without John Turner this project would not have happened as it did. Those agencies and entities did their jobs, and did them well. Turner moved outside the comfort zone of his executive position at the W.C. Bradley Company, embraced a vision, and pulled all those agencies along with him until it became a reality.

An Urban Statesman in Action

John Turner was the key to the success of the River Restoration Project in a number of significant ways. First, he was the keeper of the vision. Turner was not the first person to envision a whitewater course in Columbus. He credits Neal Wickham and Joe Smith with the idea. But Turner was the guy who, in 1998, "dusted off the file" and decided "it was just too good of an idea to not explore. If it actually is an amazing river behind those dams, I thought at the time, we've got to do this. It's just too cool that it could be in the middle of two downtowns."[65] Not everyone agreed. His fellow W.C. Bradley Company executive Mat Swift was dubious at best. "I'll put it to you this way," says Swift. "The first time I heard of that whitewater project, busting up two dams, I said, 'He's crazy. Don't even include me in this.'" But Turner persisted, and got himself appointed as head of an investigatory committee—and Swift went on to become one of his best fund-raisers.

That is in large part because Turner, from 1998 until the project was declared a "go" in 2010, approached the project as an explorer, not as an advocate. He did not adopt the project and try to sell it. Instead, he proceeded from the assumption that it would be "too

---

[65] Tony Adams, "Whitewater Project's Top Proponent Reflects on Long Journey to Get Chattahoochee Park Open," *Columbus* (GA) *Ledger-Enquirer*, 20 May 2013, http://infoweb.newsbank.com.afpls.idm.oclc.org/iw-search/we/InfoWeb, accessed 20 November 2013.

cool" if it were possible—and then explored the possibility. "It started as kind of a conversation," he says. "The very first thing we did was have a big group of people, and the engineers talked about what might be possible. It wasn't an attempt to convince. It was like, 'Well, what do y'all think' There were a lot of questions: What's it going to look like? What's it going to do to the fish? And those questions had to be answered. We had to wrap our minds around the implications of what we were doing."

Turner enlisted the help of experts—John Anderson and Rick McLaughlin for whitewater course design, Jim Phillips from Chattahoochee Riverkeeper for environmental issues, Glen Coffee from the Army Corps of Engineers for technical issues—to ensure he and other decision makers had adequate information. He asked for and received support from the Chamber of Commerce and a whole collection of civic organizations when he needed their endorsement or expertise. He searched for funding sources—the Bradley-Turner Foundation and the Army Corps of Engineers were two of his favorites—who were interested in answering the questions he was asking. The result was often a simple answer to a complex problem. Turner gave an example in an interview with *Ledger-Enquirer* in May 2013:

> [In 2002] and again in 2004, the Corps of Engineers identified a need at the approximate location of the TSYS island, we call it. At low flow that whole area was going to be essentially de-watered, and that would happen every day. There's a slough through there and it's called the habitat pool. That area was identified as being really important because there are so many nesting birds.... We didn't want to do anything to screw that up. We needed to create this habitat pool, and the way we intended to do that was to build some structures from the Alabama side of the river—where the main flow of the river wanted to flow—and that would push water back into that area.... A pretty important change of plans came when we decided to, rather than jack the river up on the Alabama side, take the river down on the Georgia side. So we did a little bit of excavation to get water back into

the Georgia side, at one-twentieth the cost, and it literally was the thing that saved the project. The other plan would have spent our entire budget just trying to get water over there.

A similar "what are the possibilities?" approach helped when it was discovered that breaching City Mills Dam would lower the water level in front of an upstream dam, resulting in damage to the turbines. A weir, now called the Bibb Dam, was constructed to solve that problem.[66]

Turner also had an uncanny ability to bring together people who normally saw themselves as being on opposite sides of most issues. He and his fellow Columbus and Phenix City business executives, as well as the political communities of both Columbus and Phenix City, saw the whitewater project as an economic development project with recreational overtones. The Army Corps of Engineers was not into recreation, but they had funding available for projects that restored ecosystems along waterways around the nation. The National Oceanic and Atmospheric Administration had funds available through their Open Rivers Initiative, which targets removal of man-made dams to improve habitat along rivers and streams.[67] The River Restoration Project served two aims, and Turner appealed to both sides.

This ability to pull diverse interests together was part of what made Turner such an extraordinary fund-raiser and advocate once the decision to go forward with the project was made. When he spoke to Columbus business executives at W.C. Bradley, Aflac, and TSYS, he argued that whitewater would make Columbus the type of city that would attract the workforce they needed. When he presented plans to the city governments of Columbus and Phenix City, he talked about economic development. The proposals he developed for the Corps of Engineers addressed issues of conservation and

---

[66] Ibid.

[67] Adams, "$24.4 Million Chattahoochee River Restoration Project a Blend of Public, Private Funding," 6 April 2013.

environmental health. The result was that few of these funding sources saw any reason to turn him down. The level of contribution was unusually high.

Finally, Turner was a consistent, calm, and upbeat voice for the River Restoration Project. He chaired both the Fall Line Alliance and the Chattahoochee River Restoration Committee. Seldom did a newspaper article about the project appear where Turner was not quoted. Even during the slow years when the Corps of Engineers was distracted and federal funding was slow to appear, Turner stayed on message: things were proceeding slowly—but they were proceeding. The *Ledger-Enquirer* consistently identified Turner as the project's "leader"—"the driving force"—the "chief advocate"—"the project's champion since the conceptual phase" who had "spearheaded [the project] for more than a decade." When someone wanted to know something about the status of the whitewater project, John Turner was the person to whom they turned.

As a result, while politicians and business executives, environmentalists and bureaucrats, kayakers, and engineers all played important roles in bringing Columbus's whitewater course to life, it is safe to say that no single individual had a bigger role in the project than John Turner, and that it would not have been the same without him.

Where Next?

How was the whitewater project doing at the end of summer 2013, its first season of operation? There was still a bit of construction happening. In July a new put-in below the North Highland Dam and a new rapid at the top of the course, named Ambush, opened.[68] There was still some debris-removal from the dam breaches going on in

---

[68] Mike Owen, "New Rapid Added to Chattahoochee Whitewater Course; Full Course Could Open July 4," *Columbus* (GA) *Ledger-Enquirer*, 29 June 2013, http://infoweb.newsbank.com.afpls.idm.oclc.org/iw-search/we/Info-Web, accessed 26 August 2013.

parts of the river.[69] But the river run was basically finished, and it was a rousing success. In fact, *USA Today* named the course to its "Built to Thrill" list—twelve of the greatest man-made adventures on the planet.[70] (John Turner's only distress was that they called course "man-made." He gives credit to the river.)

In its first four months, more than 16,000 people rode down the river on a Whitewater Express raft in spite of a Fourth of July weekend washout, when rain and high water forced the course to close. The outfitters and Uptown Columbus were initially distressed and embarrassed by a YouTube video showing a multi-raft pile-up at high flow on Cut-Bait, the Class IV+ rapid downstream from the Eagle & Phenix Dam on the Alabama side, then realized that the resulting 140,000-plus views of the video provided some excellent free publicity.[71] Whitewater Express owner Dan Gilbert anticipates a sharp increase in business over the next two years, predicting 25,000 to 40,000 rafters in 2014 and "flirting with 100,000" by 2015.[72] The course is open year-round, although the bulk of the action is expected to take place between March and October.

In the meantime, Columbus is leveraging the excitement generated by Whitewater as it moves to the next step in revitalizing downtown. Columbus State University hopes to partner with private

---

[69] Chuck Williams, "Construction Crew Clears Debris from Whitewater Course," *Columbus* (GA) *Ledger-Enquirer*, 22 October 2013, http://infoweb.newsbank.com.afpls.idm.oclc.org/iw-search/we/InfoWeb, accessed 23 October 2013.

[70] "Whitewater Gets Great Advertising Money Can't Buy," *Columbus* (GA) *Ledger-Enquirer*, 29 August 2013, http://infoweb.newsbank.com.afpls.idm.oclc.org/iw-search/we/InfoWeb, accessed 16 September 2013.

[71] Chuck Williams, "First Season of Chattahoochee River Whitewater Rafting Attracts More Rafters Than Anticipated," *Columbus* (GA) *Ledger-Enquirer*, 3 October 2013, http://infoweb.newsbank.com.afpls.idm.oclc.org/iw-search/we/InfoWeb, accessed 23 October 2013.

[72] Chuck Williams, "First Run at Whitewater Has Drawn 7,5000 Rafters," *Columbus* (GA) *Ledger-Enquirer*, 22 July 2013, http://infoweb.newsbank.com.afpls.idm.oclc.org/iw-search/we/InfoWeb, accessed 26 August 2013.

interests to renovate the old newspaper building and move its nursing and education programs downtown—bringing even more activity to the area. University president Dr. Tim Mescon shamelessly promotes his university with images of students traveling down the river in rafts stamped with the university logo. "Mr. Bill" Turner is promoting plans for a dancing fountain on the riverfront and a veteran's memorial park.

John Turner observes that while Columbus "has a Riverwalk, it doesn't yet really have a riverfront," so there's lots of room for development. Across the river in Phenix City, Troy State University is developing riverfront property, and W.C. Bradley Real Estate is developing a shopping district. Whitewater is paying off big time, says Turner: "We've spent the money and this is going to be an investment that pays dividends forever. The river is transformed and there's not the need to keep plowing more and more money into it to kind of sustain it. If you want to talk about whether the community is getting good value out of this, I don't think the math is hard at all."[73]

---

[73] Adams, "Whitewater Project's Top Proponent," 20 May 2013.

Eight Rules for Successful Urban Statesmanship

Jeffrey Hollender, president and CEO of Vermont-based cleaning products company Seventh Generation, argues, "Global and local business—private enterprise—present the largest force truly capable of providing workable solutions, not just to business problems but to the daunting social and environmental challenges facing our planet."[1] The five examples of urban statesmanship you have just seen illustrate the diversity of situations in which business leaders can have a substantial impact in the public policy arena. Clearly, a wide range of opportunities present themselves to those looking for involvement in civic leadership activities.

Just as interesting as the differences among the cases we've examined, however, are the similarities. A close examination of the work of these successful urban statesmen and the contexts in which they operate suggests a catalogue of "best practices" that provides useful guidance to the prospective statesman pondering a leadership opportunity. I've identified eight such practices.

1. Select an issue at its "tipping point"

My observation is that business leaders operating in the policy arena are most likely to have a successful experience when they are involved with an issue at or near its "tipping point." That's the point at which an issue is or is perceived to be ready to succeed or fail very shortly. Not dealt with, an opportunity will be lost, or a crisis will become irreversible. John F. Kennedy School of Government faculty

---

[1] Jeffrey Hollender and Stephen Fenichell, *What Matters Most: How a Small Group of Pioneers Is Teaching Social Responsibility to Big Business, and Why Big Business Is Listening* (New York: Basic Books, 2004) x.

members Ronald Heifetz and Marty Linsky use the term "ripe" to characterize such policy problems. "An issue is ripe," they say, "when there is widespread urgency to deal with it."[2]

This definition contains two key concepts. The first is urgency: not only is there a problem, it needs to be corrected *now* in order to seize an opportunity or to avoid a failure. Harvard Business School professor John P. Kotter outlines an eight-step change process, meant to apply to the business world but applicable to the policy sector as well. He begins with "establish a sense of urgency"—necessary, he says, to "help defrost a hardened status quo."[3] Urgency is crucial to overcoming inertia and complacency, making change both possible and attractive.

This sense of urgency may sometimes rise to the level of what Daryl Conner calls a "burning platform," creating a situation so painful that there is no acceptable alternative other than policy change.[4] Such a condition exists, he argues, when the costs— economic, social, personal and otherwise—of maintaining the current policy become greater than the costs of change. "When an organization is on a burning platform," he concludes, "the decision to make a major change is not just a good idea—it is a business imperative."[5] Grady Hospital's situation—imminent closure—is such an example.

Less dire situations can also generate sufficient urgency to inspire policy change and allow an urban statesman to make a significant contribution. "Ripeness" does not seem to require approaching disaster so much as it needs a consciousness of the relative costs and

---

[2] Ronald A. Heifetz and Marty Linsky, *Leadership on the Line: Staying Alive thorough the Dangers of Leading* (Boston: Harvard Business School Press, 2002) 146.

[3] John P. Kotter, *Leading Change* (Boston: Harvard Business School Press, 1996) 21–22.

[4] Daryl R. Conner, *Managing at the Speed of Change: How Resilient Managers Succeed and Prosper Where Others Fail* (New York: Villard Books, 1992) 93.

[5] Conner, *Managing at the Speed of Change,* 93.

benefits of the present and proposed policies. Heifetz and Linsky suggest there are four key questions one can ask to determine "when, or whether, an issue becomes ripe." They are: "What other concerns occupy the people who need to be engaged? How deeply are people affected by the problem? How much do people need to learn? And what are the senior authority figures saying about the issue?" [6] A crucial component in developing answers to these questions is how the issue at hand is treated by the media. How the various media report on an issue greatly influences whether the public is concerned about it, how much they know about it, and what the public believes its leaders think about it. The ripest issues are those where people are heavily affected by the problem and not preoccupied with other issues, understand the dimensions of the problem, and see and hear credible leadership figures supporting its solution.

By these measures, both the Oklahoma City MAPS referendum and the Salt Lake City transportation referendum responded to "tipping point" issues. While neither city would have self-destructed, particularly in the short-term, in the absence of the initiatives proposed, in both cases the issues being addressed (city image and traffic) were priorities to those affected by them; the problems were well-defined; and strong and respected leadership figures—our urban statesmen—pushed for solution.

In the case of Houston's Disaster Planning and Recovery Task Force, the initial push for disaster planning solutions reflects a potential "burning platform" situation. The city had just experienced an extremely costly hurricane and the need for a change in the disaster management process was clear and salient. To leave the disaster management process as it was risked huge costs in similar future situations—and such situations were sure to come. The farther removed from the hurricane and its damage the participants became, however, the less the urgency to propose and implement solutions— even though the task force itself admitted that it had more work to

---

[6] Heifetz and Linsky, *Leadership on the Line*, 148.

do. Small groups of those for whom the remaining issues continued to be "ripe"—Joni Baird, Francisco Sanchez and others concerned with developing an information-sharing system, for instance—continued to work outside of the task force structure to create solutions, but the task force itself lost its momentum.

John Turner faced the opposite problem in Columbus, Georgia. By 2010, when Turner and his committee decided it was time to move forward with building a whitewater course through the city, the issue had been around for years. Their challenge was to make it seem pressing in the present, particularly when it came to fund-raising. The real tipping point for Turner was the need for funds. Turner and other spokesmen for the project, particularly Mat Swift, generated the required urgency by presenting the whitewater course as the solution to a seemingly unrelated but pressing problem: attracting qualified workers to fill technology-based jobs in the city. Building the course, they argued, would make the city of Columbus more attractive to well-educated young workers who were looking for a high quality of life. A whitewater course through downtown was something these younger, better educated, more adventurous workers would expect of "a Greenville, an Austin, a Charleston, a Boulder," and finding it in Columbus would move the city to the ranks of these attractive towns.

"Widespread" is the second important concept here. In the Grady Hospital situation, for instance, it was not enough for Tom Bell and Pete Correll to believe that Grady Hospital had hit the financial wall. It wasn't even enough for them to convince me and the Board of the Metro Atlanta Chamber that we needed to consider involving ourselves in solving the problem. To make Grady a "ripe" issue, it was also necessary that the Fulton-DeKalb Hospital Authority and the county commissions of Fulton and DeKalb counties acknowledge Grady's situation, and that required encouraging their constituents to push them in that direction. The *Atlanta Journal-Constitution*, which ran frequent stories about Grady's financial situation, had a significant role in creating that "push" and giving a sense of credibility to the crisis.

Correll, Bell, and Russell faced a huge communication task, made even more difficult by the fact that Grady Hospital had a history of pleading "financial crisis" every year at budget time as it tried to pressure Fulton and DeKalb counties to increase their financial contributions to the hospital—not that the increases weren't needed. The hospital's current status had to be communicated to the public with credibility if something was to be done about the problem.

In Salt Lake City, the 2015 Alliance faced a less challenging path to the same outcome. Although they had plenty of statistical information indicating how bad traffic was in the Wasatch Valley and how much worse it would become, they also had a great advantage in selling their argument: the population that would vote in the tax referendum experienced that same traffic every day. The transportation problem had already been studied by transportation and planning professionals; they had developed a solution around which consensus had been reached. The question became quite narrow—not whether there should be new tax funding for roads and transit, but what kind of tax would be used, and when. Their issue was ripe, indeed.

Still, Salt Lake City's 2015 Alliance did face a challenge convincing the Governor to call a special legislative session to get their specific proposal on the November ballot. "Our greatest talking point," says Natalie Gochnour, "was that we were ready to go, that business supported it, and that all we were asking for was for the public to get a chance to weigh in and also that it would cost us less to go ahead. We were going to fall back about fifteen spots in the federal funding line if we couldn't go after that money now. We created a sense of urgency."[7]

Of the cases discussed here, the Columbus, Georgia whitewater project presents the most compelling evidence of widespread

---

[7] Natalie Gochnour, interview, 8 May 2012.

support. From the first endorsement of the Corps of Engineers study by the Columbus Council in 2002,[8] the project was popular with the community. By the end of the project, eighteen different governmental (local, state, and federal), business, historic preservation, environmental, and recreational organizations were involved in partnerships related to the development of the course.[9] Press support for the project was overwhelming; reporting was frequent and favorable, aside from some articles citing the concerns of fishermen[10] and the occasional "Letter to the Editor" lambasting Turner and his group as "The Committee to Pave the Chattahoochee" because the project added some man-made features to the river.[11] This near-universal positive regard for the project made its "urgency" a much easier sell.

---

[8] Chuck Williams, "Supports River Study—May Remove Dams for Kayaking, Rafting, and Fishing," *Columbus* (GA) *Ledger-Enquirer*, 22 May 2002, C-8.

[9] In a presentation on the project he made to Leadership Savannah in May 2013, Mat Swift listed the following organizations as partners in the project: Columbus Consolidated Government, Greater Columbus Chamber of Commerce, Russell County-Phenix City Chamber of Commerce, United States Army Corps of Engineers, Columbus Water Works, Historic Columbus Foundation, Uptown Columbus, East Alabama Riverfront Development, Chattahoochee RiverWatch, Historic Chattahoochee Commission, Columbus Convention and Visitors Bureau, The Nature Conservancy, Alabama Rivers Alliance, Oxbow Meadows Environmental Education Center, Georgia Department of Natural Resources, Alabama Department of Natural Resources, US Fish and Wildlife Service, and the US Canoe and Kayak Federation.

[10] See, for example, Bryan Brasher, "Fishy Plan—Some Anglers Wary of River Restoration Project," *Columbus* (GA) *Ledger-Enquirer*, 18 October 2004, A-1.

[11] Cited in Chuck Williams, "Outfitter Pulling out of Whitewater Project Leaves Us with Questions," *Columbus* (GA) *Ledger-Enquirer*, 13 May 2013, http://infoweb.newsbank.com.afpls.idm.oclc.org/iw-search/we/InfoWeb, accessed 20 November 2013.

2. Play to your strengths

In an earlier chapter I identified a number of characteristics typically possessed by those who are likely to be effective urban statesmen. The particular strengths required in individual situations, though, can vary widely. As Otis White observes, "Every complicated civic project needs a combination of talents: strategists, experts, leaders, project managers, fund-raisers, political insiders, credible spokespersons, and enthusiasts."[12] Effective urban statesmen match their strengths as leaders to the situations in which they choose to become involved. John Kotter and Dan Cohen argue that having the "right people" in charge is essential to effective change management. "By the 'right people,'" they say, "we mean individuals with the appropriate skills, the leadership capacity, the organizational credibility, and the connections to handle a specific kind of…change."[13] The urban statesman, in short, is most effective in situations where he or she is considered a skillful and credible leader.

Mae Jemison's skill as a "masterful facilitator"[14] (the phrase comes from Chevron's Joni Baird, who served on the Greater Houston Partnership's Disaster Planning and Recovery Task Force) was key to the smooth functioning of this diverse group, drawn from the private, non-profit, institutional and government sectors and full of competing interests. Likewise, a specific combination of skills—Ray Ackerman's ability to articulate a vision for Oklahoma City and Ron Norick's organizational and implementation skills—was crucial to the passage and eventual success of MAPS. In Salt Lake City, the specific skills and connections of the most active "statesmen"—Scott Anderson, Keith Rattie, Clark Ivory, Scott Parson, and Mark Howell, supported by Lane Beattie—helped define a task list for legislative

---

[12] Otis White, *The Great Project* (Apple iBook, 2012) 11.

[13] John Kotter and Dan S. Cohen, *The Heart of Change: Real-Life Stories of How People Change Their Organizations* (Boston: Harvard Business School Press, 2002) 43.

[14] Joni Baird, interview, 22 November 2011.

Those who wish to become urban statesmen would be wise to add these two strengths—open-mindedness and a willingness to take the long view—to their personal stable.

3. Find a forum

In addition to possessing the right leadership skills and attributes for the task, the urban statesman also requires support. The tasks they typically undertake require logistical and administrative support, research, media support, and wide-ranging civic and political connections. This support most often and most effectively comes from the staff of business-civic organizations such as chambers of commerce or CEO-based civic organizations, and sometimes from universities and consulting firms. Such support is crucial, says Carnegie Mellon's Rick Stafford: "Having the right civic leader willing to take responsibility for a particular outcome and having the right professional leaders...to provide support for the civic leader is a winning combination. Neither one can be successful without the other. If you intend to do something of significance, you must have both types of leaders. They will build the coalitions, bring influence to bear, and create the conditions of success."[17] The "professional leaders" Stafford references are people like me: chamber of commerce officials and paid staff members who have access to the information and logistical support urban statesmen need to accomplish their goals.

Such organizational support played a prominent role in each of the cases we've examined. The Greater Salt Lake City Chamber of Commerce, the Oklahoma City Chamber, the Metro Atlanta Chamber, the Greater Houston Partnership, the Greater Columbus Chamber, and Uptown Columbus all actively supported the efforts of the urban statesmen in our case studies. Projects originate in various

---

[17] Quoted in Frey Foundation, "The New Landscape of Civic Business: How Business Leadership is Influencing Civic Progress in Our Metropolitan Regions Today," (2012) 24.

ways. In the cases of Oklahoma City, Atlanta, and Columbus, the statesmen brought their project to the organization—Ray Ackerman through a vision-generating retreat; Tom Bell, Pete Correll and Michael Russell through a direct request for support; and John Turner in response to Neal Wickham's video. In Houston and Salt Lake City, the civic organization generated the project, recruited the statesmen to lead it, and provided ongoing support. Both approaches work.

Support from a chamber of commerce or other business or civic forum is important to the urban statesman for at least three reasons. First, the presence of such support provides credibility for the statesman's efforts. As you read earlier, Pete Correll and Tom Bell started their effort to reform Grady Hospital's governance with the Metro Atlanta Chamber because they knew sponsorship from our organization would give their effort some heft. John Turner used Uptown Columbus for the same reason; they had developed and supported a long line of projects important in the revitalization of downtown Columbus. The involvement and backing of an agency from outside of the local environment, the Army Corps of Engineers, also added credibility to the project, even as it increased the logistical problems associated with its implementation.

In Salt Lake City, given their recent history of successfully completing projects on time and under budget, the UTA and the UDOT could have pushed for a transportation tax referendum on their own. However, as former Questar chairman Keith Rattie observes, the agencies were viewed as so self-interested they were assumed to be feathering their own nests. "One thing that made this work," he notes, "was taking the messaging away from the self-interested agencies and giving the initiative a business message."[18] Commissioning an outside study and then basing the transportation referendum campaign in the business community increased the credibility of the campaign's message, improving its chance of success. Clark Ivory, CEO of Ivory Homes and one of the active urban

---

[18] Keith Rattie, interview, 9 April 2012.

statesmen in this campaign, said it quite simply: "Here in Utah, they listen to business."[19]

Forum support also helps with the urban statesman's information and logistic needs. All of the projects we have examined required substantial research and related document generation; agendas, studies, data displays, graphs, charts, and reports are the raw materials for all of these efforts. Business/civic organizations can generate this information with much greater ease and with less personal expense than can an individual campaigning for a cause. In the case of the Grady Hospital Task Force, for instance, the Metro Atlanta Chamber was able to garner pro bono support from consultants and law firms that would not likely have been available to Correll, Russell, and Bell as individuals. The Metro Atlanta Chamber has frequently used a wide variety of consultants, including, Bain, Boston Consulting Group, McKinsey, North Highland, and Cap Gemini, working on either a pro bono or paid basis, to support task-force efforts. Additionally, Chamber staff, especially our then Senior Vice-President for Public Policy Renay Blumenthal, coordinated extensive logistical support for the task force, generating agendas and informational documents for task-force meetings, and coordinating the final report with task-force leadership.

Similarly, funding and staff support from the Oklahoma City Chamber allowed the initial MAPS task force to remain out of the public eye "long enough to accomplish major brainstorming and organization of ideas."[20] The Chamber also paid for Rick Horrow, the Florida-based sports facilities consultant who helped the task force develop and publicize its plans.[21]

---

[19] Clark Ivory, interview, 2 May 2012.

[20] Bob Burke with Joan Gilmore, *Old Man River: The Life of Ray Ackerman* (Oklahoma City: Oklahoma Heritage Association, 2002) 261.

[21] Steve Lackmeyer and Jack Money, *OKC: Second Time Around* (Oklahoma City: Full Circle Press, 2006) 112–14.

Columbus, Georgia's, Fall Line Alliance, led by John Turner and operated as a study committee of Uptown Columbus, made extensive use of forums for information and logistical support. Early financial seed money from the Bradley-Turner Foundation (another of Turner's forums) paid to bring in John Anderson and Rick McLaughlin to study the river. Turner also prevailed upon the Columbus Council to sponsor a $400,000 Corps of Engineers feasibility study, involving two more existing organizations in directly supporting the project. Endorsements from civic groups—the Historic Columbus Foundation, the Chamber of Commerce, and the Chattahoochee Riverkeeper (also used by the Alliance as a source for raising early seed money) expanded the resources available to the Alliance when assistance or information was needed.

Finally, business/civic organizations offer to urban statesmen ready channels for dealing with media. The role of the media is critical in helping educate the public and building support for major change. A professional staff with experience in dealing with reporters, managing access to leaders, preparing editorials and opinion articles, managing press conferences, and dealing with critics and opponents in the public arena is an important asset. Professional staff can help screen and prioritize media requests, as well as prepare talking points and press releases to ensure a consistent message.

Natalie Gochnour, Executive Vice President for Policy and Communication for the Salt Lake City Chamber, was essential to the communication efforts of the 2015 Alliance, according to urban statesman Clark Ivory: "She coordinated that function for us. She knew how to create sound bites [for the media] as well as how to speak in paragraphs to the board, and helped us package the information so we could sell the program to both the public and the business community."[22]

Esther Campi, then our Senior Vice President for Communications, performed the same function for the Metro Atlanta Chamber

---

[22] Clark Ivory, interview, 2 May 2012.

and the Greater Grady Task Force. Pete Correll recalls, "Esther Campi and Che Watkins at the Chamber essentially worked for me during that period. They went with me everywhere. We met with editorial boards and everyone else and convinced people (a) that the problem was real, and (b) that fixing the operation of the hospital was not going to be adequate, that we had to raise capital from the philanthropic community."[23] Rick Horrow, working for the Oklahoma City Chamber, teamed with urban statesman and Oklahoma City mayor Ron Norick to convince other Oklahoma City business executives to fund the MAPS campaign.[24] Ray Ackerman, who headed an advertising agency, also worked with the Oklahoma City Chamber to create a "Believe in Our Future" advertising campaign to sell the MAPS initiative.[25]

The importance of forum support can also be defined by its absence. In the case of Houston's Disaster Planning and Recovery Task Force, three task force participants—Elaine Barber, Francisco Sanchez, and Joni Baird—and its chair, Dr. Mae Jemison, mentioned the difficulties caused by staff turnover in the personnel assigned to their project at the Greater Houston Partnership—particularly when it came to achieving the goals of the task force beyond generating a response to the Governor's Task Force Report. While none of them questioned the efforts or the good intentions of the GHP to provide adequate support for their efforts, all noted the difficulties caused by repeated turnover in the assigned staff.

4. Get invited in

Entering the public policy arena when one is not perceived to be a "public policy person"—that is to say, a politician or government official—can be difficult. At some level, the involvement of business executives in policy development is perceived as "meddling."

---

[23] Pete Correll, interview, 28 November 2011.
[24] Lackmeyer and Money, *OKC*, 124–27.
[25] See Lackmeyer and Money, *OKC*, 122 for an example.

Business people are allowed to have public opinions on business-related issues—corporate taxes, business incentives, economic-development policy—but not necessarily on education, transportation, healthcare, or stadium construction. So before representatives of the business community delve into these broader quality-of-life issues, it is important that they be asked for their opinions and involvement. They need to be invited in.

Obtaining such an invitation was particularly important to me when the Grady Hospital issue arose. I felt it was important to define why the business community should be involved. I did not want to be party to throwing the business community in general, and the Metro Atlanta Chamber in particular, into the middle of a tremendously controversial and politically explosive issue when the hospital's governing authorities—they had their own board plus direct connections to both the Fulton and DeKalb county commissions—had given no indication that they wanted us to be there. So Pete Correll and Tom Bell went looking for an invitation, contacting the leadership of the Fulton-DeKalb Hospital Authority and the two county commissions and offering our assistance if they would ask for it.

Bell, who served on the Emory Healthcare board, was connected to Pam Stephenson, chair of the Fulton-DeKalb Hospital Authority and to vice-chair Dr. Chris Edwards, so he met with them. Pete Correll and I met with the members of the Fulton County Commission and the DeKalb County CEO, Vernon Jones, who appointed the Hospital Authority Board members and were responsible for a large portion of Grady's funding. The Fulton County situation was particularly complex: each commissioner appointed a member of the Hospital Authority board, so we had to meet with the individual commissioners as well as with the chairman. Our message to these officials was, "We know you have a serious financial problem, and we think we can pull together business resources that will be helpful to you. If you will ask us for our help, we will give it." By 28 February 2007, enough folks had agreed to our involvement that an official letter of invitation from the FDHA was in hand, and a task force was then created.

The Houston task force represents a more direct form of invitation. Following the 2008 hurricane season, Texas governor Rick Perry had convened a state-level task force to study the state's response to a series of storms, including Hurricane Ike, which had devastated the Texas coast in September of that year. Wanting to include the reactions of Houston's business community in the report, he contacted Jeff Moseley, then CEO of the Greater Houston Partnership (who had previously served as Perry's Director of the Governor's Office of Economic Development and Tourism)[26] and asked that he coordinate a response to the preliminary draft of his task force's report. Moseley and the Partnership board decided a task force that included representatives of the various affected business, institutional, and governmental entities would provide the best response, and asked Dr. Mae Jemison, a GHP board member, to head the effort.

John Turner and the Fall Line Alliance faced a very different situation. First, they saw themselves as addressing an opportunity, not solving a problem. Their river was not "broken"—they simply thought they might have a way to better capitalize on an existing asset. Second, there was no one in charge of the river from whom to ask permission. Rather, they were operating in a culture, created in part by Turner's father, which for more than twenty years had looked for the "next new thing" to enhance downtown Columbus. In many ways this culture acted as Turner's invitation, particularly when what he was proposing at the early stage of the project was not action but investigation. Later on, when facing the decision about whether to

---

[26] Chris Eaton, "Greater Houston Partnership CEO Moseley to Step Down," *Houston Business Journal* (May 2012), http://www.bizjournals.com/houston/morning_call/2012/05/greater-houston-partnership-ceo.html, accessed 25 November 2013.

proceed with the project, Turner's more "official " invitation came from the city of Columbus, W.C. Bradley Company, the Bradley-Turner Foundation, TSYS, and Aflac, in the form of substantial contributions that made it possible for the project to proceed.

The other two cases we have examined were ballot initiatives, and I'd argue that any ballot initiative is an invitation for the involvement of all interested parties in the public policy sphere. Getting an issue on the ballot is sometimes the bigger issue. In Salt Lake City, members of the business community were approached by the UTA for assistance with a potential transit ballot initiative and chose to broaden the issue to include roads as a condition for their involvement. The business community then effectively lobbied the state legislature for a special session to get the tax initiative to fund the combined transportation initiative placed on the ballot. In Oklahoma City, following the loss of the proposed United Airlines maintenance facility to Indianapolis, both the business and political communities were scrambling, looking for ways to improve the city's image. Both perceived the need for a bold public initiative to rejuvenate Oklahoma City's confidence. Those two groups working together developed the initiative that became MAPS; ultimately the decision to place the MAPS initiative on the ballot came via the unanimous decision of Mayor Ron Norick and the city council.[27]

5. Do your homework

There's a saying that everyone is entitled to his own opinion, but not to his own facts. A theme that runs consistently through the five case studies we are considering is that successful urban statesmanship requires extensive fact-finding. In each case, the urban statesman involved anchored the policy change he or she proposed in comprehensive documentation of the problem being addressed.

This should not be a surprise; what executive would want to make a crucial business decision without complete information and a

---

[27] Lackmeyer and Money, *OKC*, 124.

thorough understanding of the alternatives? Carnegie Mellon's Rick Stafford applies this principle directly to the situation of the urban statesman:

> The evidence is important. The conditions that exist within a community and people's reaction to those conditions provide the case for change. So, you must provide fact-based information and observations highlighting the nature of the problem and the implications of that problem. The public will react to that. It's a key driver. Painting that picture enables a coalition of leadership to rally around that issue. Providing that information provides a platform for leaders, CEOs, to exercise their influence in moving the community toward action to address that set of conditions.[28]

The crucial information can come from a variety of sources— sometimes from internal research, sometimes from experts directly involved on task forces or in study groups, sometimes from outside consultants, sometimes even from your critics—but it is always a necessary part of the picture presented both to those who are formulating solutions to problems or evaluating opportunities and to those who will approve the policy change. Public debate focused on alternative solutions can provide additional avenues for study and essential information for weighing the impact of various alternative solutions.

Columbus, Georgia's, Fall Line Alliance may be the ultimate example of doing one's homework; its information-collection process lasted twelve years. Turner and his committee drew on a plethora of experts and organizations as they assembled the information necessary to evaluate their project. John Anderson and Rick McLaughlin, experts in designing canoeing and kayaking venues, looked at the possibility of the whitewater run as a recreational asset. The Army Corps of Engineers and a variety of state and private agencies studied the environmental implications of the proposal,

---

[28] Quoted in Frey Foundation, "The New Landscape of Civic Business," 20.

particularly as it related to fish and bird habitats. Georgia Power Company, which used the dams on the river to generate power, had another set of concerns. Historic-preservation organizations and river-protection groups were consulted. Turner was particularly skilled at identifying the crucial questions that needed to be answered to evaluate the project and gathering the information that provided the answers. The long timeline required by the Corps of Engineers gave him the time to be thorough.

The Greater Grady Task Force in Atlanta also conducted a thorough process, though in a more constricted time frame. The task force had access to in-depth studies of hospital operations conducted by consultants Alvarez and Marsal and received pro bono assistance from Deloitte Consulting, which examined the governance structure of large public hospitals across the country; the Health Policy Center at Georgia State University, which looked at the use of Grady by patients not residents of Fulton and DeKalb counties; and several Atlanta law firms, which drew up necessary agreements for the change in structure.

The information from Alvarez and Marcel told us that simply fixing the internal operations of the hospital would not generate enough revenue to solve its financial problems and helped define how much operation "gap funding" would be required once the hospital's finances were stabilized. Georgia State University's work, supplemented by additional material from the Georgia Hospital Association, made it clear that charging other counties when their citizens used Grady would not generate sufficient funds to solve the problem either. The facts they presented were critical to debunk the perception that Grady's financial problems could be solved if only suburban counties would pay for Grady's care of their citizens. The work by Deloitte Consulting gave us a template for a new structure, a 501(c)(3) corporation that would lease the hospital from the Fulton-DeKalb Hospital Authority and then run it. We used this information both to formulate our recommendations and to structure our presentations to the FDHA, the county commissions, the various citizen groups who had an interest in the Grady issue, and the media. To have any credibility with these people, we had to know what we were talking about; excellent information was key.

The other case studies we have considered show a similar pattern. In Oklahoma City, the Chamber of Commerce provided funding to hire Florida-based sports facilities consultant Rick Horrow to help develop plans for new city facilities. Thomas Keilhorn and Associates did issue polling; architectural and engineering firm Frankfurt Short Bruza helped cost out potential structures. In addition, the results of previous planning efforts—Horrow told the *Daily Oklahoman* that Oklahoma City was one of the country's "most prolifically over-studied communities"[29]—provided additional detail. Watercolor concept sketches of the prospective venues made the rounds.[30] In fact, given the level of detail used to sell the projects, it is not surprising that the community became restless and a bit irritated when it took more than two and a half years to award the first construction contract.[31] The work paid off. What had begun as an effort which polling showed to be supported by only 32 percent of the voters ended in a 54 percent victory.[32]

The Salt Lake City business leaders who organized as the 2015 Transportation Alliance under the auspices of the Chamber of Commerce commissioned an in-depth study of Salt Lake City's current and future transportation needs by consultants HNTB Corporation and Tom Warne and Associates, to add independent information to other readily available data from the UDOT and UTA. "The study," former Questar CEO Keith Rattie says, "helped create a

---

[29] John Parker, "City Election on Sales Tax Set for Dec. 14," *Daily Oklahoman*, 14 October 1993, News, 1.

[30] For examples, see Lackmeyer and Money, *OKC*, 125–28.

[31] See Lackmeyer and Money, *OKC*, 149–53; and John Rohde, "MAPS Must Pick Up the Pace," *Daily Oklahoman*, 9 March 1995, Sports, 21, for details.

[32] Lackmeyer and Money, *OKC*, 126, 129.

framework for messaging the campaign. We hammered at the economic consequences of congestion and the effect of cars on air quality because of the 'bowl' nature of the Wasatch area. Our studies looked at population trends (we are a rapidly growing area) and the consequences of continuing our present course in ways the population would recognize, like travel time. All this helped build a compelling rationale for a bigger long-term commitment to transportation."[33]

While the Salt Lake City, Atlanta, and Oklahoma City projects made extensive use of outside consultants for information gathering, the Houston Disaster Planning and Recovery Task Force employed a different structure, and, therefore, a different method for assembling information. While those three projects used chamber or business/civic organization members—business executives—as their core group, the Houston task force included in its membership agencies and institutions outside of the business community, many possessing expertise in specific areas under review by the task force and thus an excellent primary source of information. The panel also invited in experts to talk about specific issues in which they had an interest. Additionally, information generated by reviews after Hurricanes Katrina and Rita in 2005 was available to the group.

Dr. Mae Jemison saw a major function of her job as chair to be "digesting the information and then asking people to respond— legislators and disaster agency staff, for instance—and then we could brainstorm reactions. We would stop from time to time to digest what we had found as a group, which forced people to choose what was important. Our process was: 'Here are major important things; here's why that's important; here's what we need to do about it.'"[34] This process occurred both at the subcommittee and at the task force level. One effect of this "digesting" emphasis was to focus discussion on areas in which the members of the task force possessed expertise.

---

[33] Keith Rattie, interview, 9 April 2012.
[34] Mae Jemison, interview, 29 November 2011.

Another was to keep discussion targeted on what Jemison considered the key issue facing the task force: "I saw our task as identifying what would allow business to come back faster, not so much what would save citizens but what would prevent economic damage."[35]

Because the initial end product of the Houston task force was a report to the governor rather than a public campaign, the need for information intended to shape public opinion was more limited than in the other studies we have considered. In Columbus, Atlanta, Salt Lake City, and Oklahoma City, however, one additional component of information gathering was quite important. With those intensely political issues, our statesmen needed good knowledge of the political constituencies with whom they were dealing—both those supporting and those opposing their positions. Obtaining and using this information required working the political system in a way unfamiliar to many executives, who frequently have the authority to make things happen by command. We've already discussed the importance of political acumen in the successful urban statesman[36] so I won't repeat that material here. I mention it merely to emphasize that this is one more area where doing one's homework can be important.

6. Define your mission, scope of work, and timeline

Given that CEOs have tremendous demands on their time generated by their "day jobs," being specific about what is expected of them in the extracurricular world of urban statesmanship helps business leaders assess both their ability to be involved and their prospects for success. Business executives operating in the policy arena need to know what they are expected to do, and when (or by when) they are going to do it. My experience has been that busy executives are often unwilling to accept an assignment that lasts longer than six to nine months, although it is clear that several of our urban statesmen were

---

[35] Ibid.

[36] See chapter 2.

willing to make a longer-term commitment. A clearly defined task and timetable clarify for all involved the demands managing a policy change will make on participants in the effort. That's important, says Dr. Mae Jemison, because public policy work "will take more time than you think it will. You have to adjust your expectations—some people will help a lot and some will help very little. You may find you have to carry much of the load yourself."[37]

Key to successful urban statesmanship, say consultants Douglas Henton, John Melville, and Kim Walesh, is "defining the scope of decision-making to be big enough to make a difference, but bounded enough to get something done."[38] Such specific definition allows the business leaders involved to select appropriate roles for involvement and to structure their time commitments to fit their ongoing business responsibilities. In situations involving a task force or committee, all participants need to understand and buy into both the task and the timeline as defined by the leaders of the effort and any outside agencies who have requested the group's input. This means pre-established meeting schedules, clearly stated attendance and work-effort expectations, and an end-date that's clear from the beginning. Any changes in these expectations need to be renegotiated with everyone affected.

Legislative projects and ballot initiatives most clearly conform to this standard. Election dates are set by law and establish the end of a campaign timeline. Legislative sessions start and end at specific times, so those involved in a campaign know when their work will end. When a statesman's project has such a clearly defined endpoint, as in our Oklahoma City and Salt Lake City cases, a key task of the urban statesman is deciding what to ask for; their concern is with designing a solution to a problem, not so much with implementing

---

[37] Mae Jemison, interview, 29 November 2011.

[38] Douglas Henton, John Melville, and Kim Walesh, *Civic Revolutionaries: Igniting the Passion for Change in America's Communities* (San Francisco: Jossey-Bass, 2004) 53.

the change. The proposed solution is frequently a direct outgrowth of the fact-finding process described above.

In the Oklahoma City case, for instance, two key decisions defined the scope of the initial MAPS project. The first was the decision to select a limited number of projects for which the proposed tax could be spent. Eight were selected, based on polling data.[39] The second was to offer the projects to voters as a package. The mission of those supporting the MAPS initiative became to sell the entire package, and hence the sales tax supporting it, to voters. Mayor Ron Norick pushed the idea that the plan contained something for everyone, arguing to arts patrons, for instance, "Are you willing to defeat your symphony because you don't like baseball?"[40] Implementation of the projects would become the task of a separate group created by the ballot initiative, and the urban statesmen would then be able to move out of the picture.

The task of the Salt Lake City 2015 Alliance and the urban statesmen conducting its business had three phases: (1) define the transportation problem and its solution (a dedicated sales tax); (2) convince the governor to call a special session of the legislature to get the sales tax option on the ballot; and (3) convince the general public to vote for the sales tax in the general election. The Alliance created an unusually condensed timeline for itself by deciding in the early spring of 2006 (after the 2006 legislative session had ended) to push for placement of its tax initiative on the November 2006 ballot—a decision that required a special legislative session in the summer of 2006—rather than waiting to address the issue during the 2007 legislative session. After a special session was called and the initiative authorized, the group had a mere six weeks to sell the initiative to the public. As in Oklahoma City, the implementation of the solution to Salt Lake City's problem was left to the appropriate governmental agencies; the work of the urban statesmen ended with the election.

---

[39] Charles Van Rysselberge, interview, 15 December 2011.
[40] Lackmeyer and Money, *OKC*, 127.

The Atlanta, Houston, and Columbus cases, which addressed problems unconstrained by legislative or electoral timelines, required more structure from the statesmen themselves. In the case of the Grady Hospital task force, we chose to set a somewhat artificial ninety-day time limit on the work of the task force, established a monthly meeting schedule up front, and made clear that we expected attendance at, and participation in, the meetings by those who accepted our invitation to join the task force. The task force generated its report within the ninety-day schedule, recommending a change in the structure of the board operating the hospital. The question then became, "What happens now?"

Our answer: Though most of the task force packed up and went back to their day jobs, our three urban statesmen stayed in the trenches until the change was in place. "We knew going in we were going to finish," Tom Bell remembers. "Most task forces define a problem and suggest an approach to a solution and then someone else comes in and does it. Here, there was no one else to do the implementation, and if there was no implementation we would have had failure—a messed-up medical system." [41] Pete Correll became, and still is, the chair of the new Grady board; Tom Bell and Michael Russell also serve on the board, as do I. Bell has headed up the Grady Foundation's fund-raising effort. In this model, specific personal commitments from the urban statesmen involved led them to work beyond the scope of the original task-force charge.

In Houston, the initial task of the Disaster Planning and Recovery Task Force was clearly defined—respond to the Governor's task force report—and the timeline, while not specific was clear enough: respond quickly. The task force was gathered, divided into subcommittees inspired by the structure of the Governor's Task Force Report, and quickly went to work, meeting in subcommittees twice a month and then as a committee of the whole once a month for four months, at which point they generated a response. The initial mission

---

[41] Tom Bell, interview, 2 December 2011.

was achieved, the scope of work accomplished as defined, and the timeline met.

Frustrating the Houston task-force leadership, though, was the fact that at an early meeting the group agreed to expand their task (with the apparent concurrence of the members) to include a broader study of disaster planning and relief in the greater Houston area. The task force designed and distributed a survey to Houston-area businesses, attempting to assess the impact of Hurricane Ike on their operations. Few responded.[42] "The further we got from the actual disaster the harder it was to maintain interest," observed task-force member Francisco Sanchez."[43] Several groups growing out of the task force continue to work on specific projects, but the task force itself has not reconvened nor has it generated any additional recommend-dations.

When it comes to timelines and expectations, the Columbus project is unique. While John Turner and the two committees that managed the project locally were active at the beginning and the end of the project, the decade-long middle portion was largely controlled by the Army Corps of Engineers, and timelines were nebulous at best. The Fall Line Alliance and Uptown Columbus handled several of the "sub-projects"—for example, obtaining the endorsement of the Corps for Engineers feasibility study from the Columbus Council and the acquisition of the dams—with distinct scope, mission, and timelines, and Turner's long-term personal commitment to the project held it together and kept it moving forward. Turner's insistence that the project was an ongoing investigation of the possibilities—"a conversation, not a sales pitch"—kept the time pressure minimal until the decision was made in 2010 to move forward with the project.

In April 2010, when "Ready2Raft" was formally inaugurated, the Columbus whitewater project took on the time, scope, and mission management characteristics of our other cases. Turner announced a

---

[42] Elaine Barber, interview, 22 September 2011.

[43] Francisco Sanchez, interview, 13 December 2011.

two-year timetable, with construction to begin in May 2011. The actual implementation of the construction plan became the job of Uptown Columbus and its project manager, Billy Turner. John Turner remained involved and committed, though, heading up the River Restoration Project Committee overseeing the project for Uptown, and leading the fund-raising effort that paid for the construction. The decommissioning of the dams and construction permitting processes delayed the start of construction until August 2011, but once the digging began, the two-year timetable held and the whitewater course opened 25 May 2013. Like Pete Correll, Michael Russell, and Tom Bell, John Turner was committed until the project was complete.

7. Create a clear, simple action plan

At the conclusion of every public-policy study in which he or she engages, an urban statesman needs to be able to answer the question, "What should happen now?" The answer needs to be clear and simple and able to survive public scrutiny from critics and the media. Complexity is an enemy. Regardless of the amount of work that went into formulating the recommendation of the task force or creating the solution proposed by the study group, and regardless of how complicated the issue being addressed may be, the effective urban statesman must be able to articulate clearly and briefly, in terms all the stakeholders can understand, what the problem is, how and why his or her plan will solve that problem, and how this plan stacks up against any alternatives. In the language of the "burning platform" metaphor, we need to know "how the remedy will eliminate the pain."[44]

The Grady Hospital reorganization illustrates the point. Pete Correll developed a clear and simple argument in support of the governance change for the hospital proposed by the Greater Grady Task Force: "(a) [Grady's financial problem] was real. (b) Fixing the

---

[44] Daryl R. Conner, *Leading at the Edge of Chaos* (New York: John Wiley & Sons, 1998) 249.

operations of the hospital was not going to provide adequate funds. We had to raise capital from the philanthropic community because we couldn't raise it from government; they were out of money too. (c) We had to change the form of governance because nobody in their right mind was going to give money to that governing organization which was appointed by the county commissioners, totally political, and it had mismanaged the place. So we proposed the 501(c)(3) board concept."[45] The actual solution was, of course, not that simple. It took hours and hours of work to develop a lease acceptable to the hospital authority, the two county commissions, a variety of involved political figures, and the task force (represented by Pete and Tom Bell). But Pete crafted what was, in effect, an elevator speech to sell a clear and specific proposal, and it worked. A complicated harangue about the ins and outs of the lease structure would have convinced few people and sent most running for the hills.

John Turner's strategy was similar, although, instead of starting with a problem, he addressed his plan as an opportunity. The Chattahoochee River was an incredible asset and, returned to a more natural state, could bring significant economic benefit to the cities of Columbus and Phenix City, Alabama, he argued. The plan itself was simple, though, as with Grady Hospital, its implementation was not. The Eagle & Phenix and City Mills dams would be taken down, and a 2.5-mile, engineered whitewater course that utilized the river's natural flow constructed. Studies showed the new course would create jobs, generate tourism, bring in substantial revenue, and enhance the river's ecology.[46] When the presentation moved out of the newspaper and into the fund-raising arena, Turner and his cohort added a wrinkle: Whitewater would make Columbus an appealing

---

[45] Pete Correll, interview, 28 November 2011.

[46] Tim Chitwood, "Update: Proponents Say Columbus' $23 Million Chattahoochee River Whitewater Project's Ready to Launch," *Columbus* (GA) *Ledger-Enquirer*, 26 April 2010, http://infoweb.newsbank.com.afpls.idm. oclc.org/iw-search/we/InfoWeb, accessed 1 May 2013.

and vibrant place to live, attracting the kind of young, energetic workers Columbus businesses needed. The plan was simple and effective, even though the construction was quite complex.

Clearly structured solutions to specific problems also served the urban statesmen of Oklahoma City and Salt Lake City well, although the two jurisdictions arrived at specificity from different directions. Oklahoma City's MAPS ballot initiative was very specific, listing eight projects for which the dedicated sales tax could be used. "The tax is absolutely limited to 5 years and absolutely earmarked for the projects we will vote on," declared pre-election publicity.[47] Should all the projects be completed before the five-year term of the tax expired, the tax would discontinue; if the five-year limit arrived and the projects were not complete, another vote would be required to continue the tax. The pre-vote campaign, themed "Believe in Our Future," was also very specific about the problems the redevelopment of Oklahoma City was expected to solve. "Do we compete with other cities for new businesses and jobs by investing in new and remodeled facilities for education, recreation tourism, sports and the arts, or do we just stop trying?" campaign materials asked. "Will we compete or will we retreat?"[48]

In Salt Lake City, the problem—impending transportation gridlock—had been defined by existing long-range transportation plans. The goal of the 2015 Alliance was to speed up the implementtation of the plans with regard to both transit and roads by making dedicated funds available ahead of the schedule posited by the 2030 Transportation Plan. High on the priority list were building four extended TRAX light rail lines, extending the Frontrunner commuter rail system, and building an alternative and parallel highway to I-15 through the Wasatch Valley. Discussion of moving up the construction timetable focused on these projects.

---

[47] Lackmeyer and Money, *OKC*, 122.
[48] Ibid.

The ballot question did not specify the projects for which the transportation dollars were to be spent, other than to say 25 percent of the funds must be used for land acquisition. The language of the question was rather vague, designating the funds for "corridor preservation, congestion mitigation or to expand capacity for transportation of regional significance,"[49] and the lack of specificity was deliberate, to allow various counties to use funds for needs they identified.

But the debate prior to placing the tax on the ballot gave voters a sense of security about how the funds would be used. In a pre-election editorial addressing the question of fund use, the *Salt Lake Tribune* argued: "In fact, the ballot doesn't say anything specific about any project, but instead speaks vaguely.... The Legislature must shoulder the blame for this, but it is vital that voters keep their eyes on the prize.... The mayors on the [Salt Lake County Council of Governments that will actually decide to impose the tax] support the TRAX lines and commuter rail. Some members of the County Council will change with the election, but the support for rail is strong there as well. These officials know that the people want these projects. Elected officials will pay a political price if they renege."[50] The arguments were apparently convincing; the initiative passed with 64 percent of the vote.[51]

The Houston Disaster Planning and recovery Task Force faced a different sort of task, because it faced a different sort of audience. Rather than addressing the public, its initial audience was the

---

[49] Matt Canham, "Sales tax for transportation debated," *Salt Lake Tribune*, 19 September 2006, http://archive.sltrib.com/printfriendly.php?id=4362295&itype-NGPSID, accessed 9 July 2012.

[50] "Vote for Prop. 3 sales-tax increase vital to transit and roads," *Salt Lake Tribune*, 22 October 2006, http://archives.sltrib.com/printfriendly.php?id=4529762&itype+NGPSID, accessed 9 July 2012.

[51] "Tax boost for transit gets big thumbs up," *Salt Lake Tribune*, 7 November 2006, http://archive.sltrib.com/printfriendly.php?id=4618531&itype=NGPSID, accessed 9 July 2012.

governor and his disaster task force. The "action plan" it needed to generate was an application of the Governor's Task Force Report to the specific situation experienced by the Greater Houston business community. For each of the report's observations and recommendations, the Houston task force needed to answer a series of questions: Does this observation/recommendation apply to the Greater Houston business community? If so, do we agree or disagree? If we agree, how would we implement this recommendation?

The five recommendations offered by the Houston task force in response to these questions comprised their report and constituted their recommended plan of action to the governor. The Houston group elected to organize their report around their own recommendations rather than respond specifically to each of the proposals contained in the Governor's Task Force Report. This strategy allowed them to simplify the structure of their report and to focus clearly on items particularly important to their local constituency, the Houston business community, such as the business communication network.

One final note, the words "clear" and "simple" are important here. The action plan that an urban statesman issues needs to be easily understandable. Unless you are dealing only with technical people, technical language and/or jargon are not helpful when it comes to presenting your plan, and may in fact cost you support. I agree with Harvard Professor John Kotter who notes, "Focused, jargon-free information can be disseminated to large groups of people at a fraction of the cost of clumsy, complicated communication. Technobabble and MBA-speak just get in the way, creating confusion, suspicion, and alienation."[52]

8. Be transparent with the public and the press

When operating in the public policy arena, transparency is a must. Openness with the public and the press creates a sense of trust and

---

[52] Kotter, *Leading Change*, 89.

credibility that is crucial to the success of the urban statesman. As Harvard Business School professor and former Medtronic CEO Bill George observes, "The key to handling public issues is to be open, straightforward, and transparent. In a crisis...observers are extremely sensitive to any attempts to dissemble or hide the truth. These will quickly be exposed, especially if subsequent events reveal your statements to be inaccurate or misleading."[53] Not only will openness keep you out of trouble; it has the potential to win you some friends. George continues: "When you are open, you are in a better position to ask people for their support. If things get worse, as they often do, people are more sympathetic to your point of view if you have kept them fully informed."[54]

Four of our five case studies reflect situations involving intense media scrutiny. The ballot initiatives in Salt Lake City and Oklahoma City received exhaustive media analysis and commentary from both a news-reporting and editorial perspective—not surprising since a public vote was required. In both cases, the business leaders involved in promoting the initiative were frequently cited as sources. While counterarguments were presented and alternatives were explored there was never a suggestion that the executives were providing anything other than full disclosure—with one exception. In Oklahoma City, the decision as to which projects would be included in the MAPS referendum was made out of the public eye. Having decided on an "all or nothing" approach (the projects were to be voted on as a unit), Mayor Ron Norick and his task force wanted to put their proposal together before presenting it to the press, rather than give the media a *de facto* voice in what projects would appear on the ballot. [55] The decision as to which projects to include, however,

---

[53] Bill George, *7 Lessons for Leading in Crisis* (San Francisco: Jossey-Bass, 2009) 91.

[54] Ibid., 92

[55] Lackmeyer and Money, *OKC*, 115.

was not made in a vacuum; as I noted earlier, extensive public polling informed the task force's selection.

Though no public vote was involved, the Columbus project was managed in very much the same way. Beginning with the presentation of the issue to the Columbus Council in 2002, newspapers covered the project in detail. Members of the Fall Line Alliance—principally John Turner but others was well—provided information about the current state of the project on request—even if the message was, "things are moving slowly, but they ARE moving." Once the project became "official," coverage continued, emphasizing progress and next steps—particularly when it came to "blowing the dams." While Turner was still the main spokesperson once construction began the *Ledger-Enquirer* turned more often to management ranks of Uptown Columbus, particularly Richard Bishop and Billy Turner, for detailed progress reports.

The Grady Task Force in Atlanta faced some particularly tricky communications issues, given that any issue related to Grady Hospital was perceived to have racial overtones. That is at least one of the reasons Michael Russell, head of the largest African-American construction firm in the city, stepped up and volunteered to serve on the task force. His presence was important. "I like to think I had the credibility, that people knew I didn't have an agenda of any sort and would bring some credibility to the fact that this effort was really an effort just to make sure that Grady survived,"[56] he reflected afterward. Although the task force itself was diverse and racially balanced, having Michael at the top served to give the group an important link to Atlanta's African-American community.

Putting an African American in the position of task force chair, however, did not make all the racial issues go away. The Rev. Tim McDonald, who frequently spoke for an opposition group called the Grady Coalition, explains: "The [Fulton-DeKalb Hospital Authority] was predominantly African-American. They were the ones running

---

[56] Michael Russell, interview, November 28, 2011

Grady at the time. And we were not convinced that these corporate leaders, the business leaders, would have the interests of poor patients [in mind]. They were seeing themselves as these nice guys who were coming to save Grady: 'We're fixing to raise all this money.' But the issue of Grady was not just money and we wanted them to understand that."[57] The way we chose to deal with racial issues as they arose, was, as Pete Correll says, "to confront them head on—to always say, 'This is a serious race issue.'" [58] Another of his favorite lines was, "This is not a black issue or a white issue; this is a green issue. This is about money."

Correll constantly found himself in close-up discussions with influential African-American leaders and having to talk about the fact that he was a white man dealing with a hospital considered to be an African-American institution. Here's how he describes those conversations:

> I went to see Reverend Lowry; I met with him one on one. I met with the Concerned Black Clergy. I had umpteen meetings with Rev. Tim McDonald, who at that time was head of the Grady Coalition. [I met with] lots of the black leaders, talking about things straight up...and I promised them that in spite of what they thought I was not a racist, that we were going to have an integrated management team, and that we were going to have an integrated board—but unfortunately I was white and I was leading the charge.[59]

For me, that pretty well defines "transparency."

Like the initiatives in Salt Lake City, Oklahoma City, and Columbus, the efforts of the group were closely covered by the media from the time the Grady task force began its work until the actual implementation of the new governing structure a year later. In January 2008, Grady's situation was even covered in the *New York*

---

[57] Grady Health Foundation, "The Grady Miracle," (video), http://www.gradyhealthfoundation.org, accessed 25 March 2013.

[58] Pete Correll, interview, 28 November 2011.

[59] Ibid.

Times. All of the task-force meetings were open and attended by the press. Those meetings and Grady board meetings frequently drew protestors; at one point we were even serving coffee and doughnuts to demonstrators outside the Chamber offices. But our goal was always to make sure that, in so far as was possible, the public, including those who opposed us, had full information. Esther Campi's ability to respond to the media and have Pete Correll and Tom Bell or Michael Russell available for personal interviews helped out public credibility. I still believe that is a big reason the African-American community—in particular, the black clergy—accepted and supported our recommendations.

It is also possible to conduct a public-policy initiative with no press participation, although the willingness to be open and transparent needs always to be part of the effort's structure. The Houston Task Force on Disaster Planning and Recovery attracted no attention in the Houston papers, in spite of its wide-ranging membership, and in spite of the fact that Hurricane Ike received substantial attention. (Searching the *Houston Chronicle* database turns up nearly a thousand articles on "Hurricane Ike" during the months the task force was most active.) Lack of attention did not prevent the group from tackling and completing its primary mission: responding to the Governor's Task Force report. Task force member Elaine Barber indicates the group had hoped for a more public face in the long run. "We did not address the initial findings from the report with the media," she remembers. "It was our plan to have the final report approved by the [GHP] board of directors and accepted and then submit it for media consumption—that did not happen."[60] Perhaps more media attention would have encouraged the task force to continue and complete its work.

---

[60] Elaine Barber, email to Laura A. Poe, 14 January 2013.

Conclusion

As I conclude this discussion, let me return for a moment to my starting place: the definition of urban statesmanship. I've talked about the urban statesman as a business executive involved in public-policy issues, using business skills and practices to research, develop, and sometimes implement solutions to public-sector problems. In the course of my seventeen years as president of the Metro Atlanta Chamber, I have watched numerous urban statesmen in action. The Chamber has fielded task forces on multiple issues, including transportation, water-resource management, and education, as well as a variety of economic-development issues including bio-sciences, wireless mobility, sustainable industries, global trade, health-information technology, clinical trials, and advanced manufacturing. All were led by business executives. The practices I've outlined in this chapter have been consistently employed by the urban statesmen I have seen in action. It's been exciting to discover that these same principles apply in other settings as well.

In summary, to accomplish their missions successfully, urban statesmen consistently employ a group of "best practices." These include:

1. Selecting an issue at its "tipping point"
2. Playing to personal strengths
3. Finding a sponsoring forum
4. Getting "invited in" to the problem-solving process
5. Doing one's homework
6. Defining the mission, scope of work, and timeline of the endeavor
7. Creating a clear, simple action plan
8. Being transparent with the public and the press.

These operational methods that, in my experience, define successful urban statesmanship, apply to a wide variety of situations. Certainly they are common to the five very diverse situations studied here. Before a potential urban statesman decides that all of these practices are within his or her competence and prepares to take on urban statesmanship full throttle, however, there is one more topic to consider: Urban statesmanship is not without its perils.

9

Cautionary Tales

Urban statesmanship can be a risky business. Carelessly conducted, involvement in the sphere of public policy can open the business executive to credibility attacks, conflicts of interest, and (less threatening but no less annoying) great frustration. I've highlighted most of these common stumbling blocks for urban statesmen as we moved through our case studies, but I'd like to take the time to mention them specifically in the context of raising a caution flag. When business executives decide to engage the world of public policy—and I encourage them to do so—they need to be aware that there are pitfalls.

Caution #1: Avoid corporate conflicts of interest

Any time business leaders take on a political issue—particularly an issue with controversy swirling around it—they run the risk of creating a point of conflict with the corporate world, a world that represents their major responsibility and demands their loyalty. After the work of the Grady Hospital task force was finished, I remember Pete Correll—who, as I have said, had retired as CEO of Georgia-Pacific and was heading his own equity firm—telling me he could not have handled such controversial issues while the CEO of a public company. "The demonstrators would have run out there in front of Wal-Mart and urged people to boycott Brawny paper towels, and Georgia-Pacific would have jerked me out of that chair and I wouldn't have been able to do anything," he said. Tom Bell deferred to Correll when it came to heading the task force because Correll was not the head of a public company, and Bell was. The issue was too hot for Bell to handle from a position of leadership, though he was willing to dedicate himself to it behind the scenes. For Michael Russell, who was on the opposite side of the racial politics, siding with the "white business community" had a different set of risks. His personal credibility in the African-American community was on the line.

Several chapters ago I wrote that Salt Lake City businessman Keith Rattie, when deciding whether to become involved in a public issue, considers whether he can defend his actions in front of institutional investors. It is important that business leaders consider whether their involvement in promoting a public-policy change will create a problem with a board of directors or with shareholders—or for a company's public image. There are many issues out there; some are controversial and some are not. I am not arguing that business leaders should not follow their consciences in involving themselves in a controversial issue, but I would encourage leaders never to take such an action without awareness of the problems they might be creating for either themselves or for the company.

A related concern is matching the level of civic involvement the leader desires to the level that his or her company is willing to sanction. The Frey Foundation, the Brookings Institution, and consultant FutureWorks have all noted that as companies become larger and more global in their orientation, the involvement of corporate executives in community issues has declined. [1] The Brookings Institution, in its 2006 paper on corporate citizenship and

---

[1] See the Frey Foundation, "Taking Care of Civic Business: How Formal CEO-Level Business Leadership Groups Have Influenced Civic Progress in Key American Cities," (1993), and "The New Landscape of Civic Business," (2012); George Washington Institute of Public Policy, "Corporate Citizenship and Urban Problem Solving: The Changing Civic Role of Business Leaders in American Cities" (Brookings Institution Metropolitan Policy Program, September 2006); and FutureWorks, "Minding Their Civic Business: A Look at the New Ways Regional Business-Civic Organizations are Making a Difference in Metropolitan North America," (Arlington MA, 2004) cited in chapter 2.

urban problem solving, suggests three reasons for this: (1) Because they are transient, regional executives feel more attachment to the corporation and to their careers than to the community in which they currently find themselves. (2) Also because they are transient, corporate executives may possess little familiarity with community institutions. The result is that "their effectiveness in problem solving thus rests on the quality of their briefings, pre-meeting negotiations, and post-event follow-through by staff. Their roles have shifted from substantive to symbolic, and from fashioning policies and solutions to bestowing legitimacy on or championing decisions formulated by professional staff."[2] In short, they feel less necessary to the process of civic problem solution, so civic involvement becomes a less appealing use of their limited time. (3) CEOs of regional offices or corporate divisions sometimes lack the autonomy to dictate their level of involvement.[3] All of these factors have made the involvement of corporate executives in civic issues more cumbersome.

Not all corporations erect such barriers; in Atlanta some of our largest corporate citizens are among the most involved (Coca-Cola Enterprises, Home Depot, and Delta Air Lines being prime examples). Support from other corporate leaders in a community can also bolster the role of the CEO statesman. This team approach to civic leadership can be promoted through recognized community leadership groups or executive leadership organizations, which can then provide "cover" to executives who choose civic projects with controversial elements.

As I've already observed, the culture of a community may well affect how involved its corporate citizens choose to be, and corporate culture, in many instances, still values community involvement. But any corporate executive inclined toward civic service should be aware of corporate policies toward such involvement and either tailor

---

[2] George Washington Institute of Public Policy, "Corporate Citizenship and Urban Problem Solving," 16.

[3] Ibid., 15–16.

his or her involvement to a level or an issue the corporation sanctions, or discuss planned involvement with someone who has the authority to approve it.

Caution #2: Watch out for "turf protectors"

I've said previously that it is important for business to "get invited in" to civic problem-solving activities. Turf protection is what tends to happen when business pokes its nose into someone else's issue without an invitation—or sometimes even when an invitation is forthcoming.

Brian Ferguson, retired CEO and chairman of Eastman Chemical Company, provides an example of turf protection in action. Eastman Chemical Company is located in an area of northeastern Tennessee known as the Tri-Cities, comprising the cities of Kingsport (Eastman's location), Johnson City, and Bristol. The three towns have long been in competition with one another when it comes to business development, but occasionally cooperative efforts emerge. One of these was the Tri-Cities Business Alliance, a group of plant managers and business executives who gathered monthly to discuss business issues. As the area's economy slowed in the late 1990s and early 2000s, three of the executives who participated in this group, including Ferguson, became interested in taking a larger, regional approach to attracting business to the area. Backed by these executives, the group hired a consultant to conduct a study of the idea. The consultant put together a proposal; the group announced the formation of an organization called the Regional Alliance for Economic Development, hired another consultant to raise funds, and hired an organization president. Ferguson was elected the first chairman of the group, which launched in 2005.[4]

What happened next was...nothing. Ferguson, who freely admits economic development is not his area of expertise, identifies two problems that stalled the fledgling organization in its tracks. First, he

---

[4] Andy Burke, interview, 16 November 2011.

says, he didn't do his homework: "I did not appreciate going in how important it was to have a store of things to sell [to the businesses we were attempting to recruit]—things like industrial parks and infrastructure. All we had was open land and not all that much of that." Second, Ferguson concedes that he had no idea he was invading the turf covered by a number of local economic development organizations—a culture that had very little interest in cooperative efforts. "The history of cooperation between business and the economic development community in this region is mixed and unhappy," he says now. "The individual cities and counties all have their own economic development groups, as does TVA, and there's something called RIDA (Regional Industrial Development Authority). In the most successful models all these entities would give up their knives and work together. Businesses that cross boundaries (and most of them do) would try to unite." But this was not the situation Ferguson faced: "We were more *Friday Night Lights*. It was really a zero-sum game around here. They were always looking for something for Kingsport or Johnson City or Bristol—'I win; you lose.' There was never a push to get, for instance, a big warehouse at the major interstate exit that would benefit everybody. I did not appreciate the depth of the rivalries. It was naïve to think that an outsider business guy could change that."[5]

Andy Burke, the first president/CEO of the Regional Alliance, suggests the economic development entities connected with the cities and counties perceived both a threat and an insult, even though neither was intended. "The Alliance was 'announced,'" he says, " as though the 'big guys' were telling the local economic development folks 'we're going to show you how to do this,' or at least it was perceived that way. The local economic development folks never supported the effort."[6] Although Ferguson regards his personal involvement in the organization as a failure, in the long run the effort

---

[5] Brian Ferguson, interview, 7 December 2011.
[6] Andy Burke, interview, 16 November 2011.

was not without its benefits. In the end, he says, "we gave the organization over to the county [executives] and the city governments. It seemed to be an issue better dealt with from a political than a business standpoint. The organization is still in place and is doing better now."[7]

Ferguson's experience illustrates the perils of entering someone else's turf uninvited, but even with an invitation, tackling a controversial issue can raise the hackles of those who see a business presence in their arena as a threat. I saw this happen in the challenges faced by the Grady task force—particularly in our relationships with the Grady Coalition and the Concerned Black Clergy. As I have indicated, the Rev. Tim McDonald, an important leader of both organizations, initially saw the work of the Greater Grady Task Force as a power play and an attempt by corporate Atlanta to take over Grady Hospital.[8] He and State Senator Vincent Fort attended task-force meetings and Grady board meetings, lead demonstrations outside the Metro Atlanta Chamber offices, and held multiple press conferences protesting the "privatization" of the hospital and the composition of the (as yet unannounced) new board.

McDonald and Fort argued their chief concern was that, in our effort to solve Grady's financial problems, we would forget the mission of the hospital: to provide safety-net healthcare to Atlanta's poor. We consistently reiterated a basic position: that we had been asked to help the hospital find a solution to its financial problems; that we had held open meetings as we arrived at our recommendations, that we were helping to raised money from philanthropic, business, and government sources to help the hospital, and that we agreed with Grady's mission. In spite of such consistent communication, it took the meeting with the Concerned Black Clergy described earlier and Pete Correll's absolute promise that the mission

---

[7] Brian Ferguson, interview, 7 December 2011.
[8] Grady Health Foundation, "The Grady Miracle," (video).

of the hospital would not change and that the board and the governing authority would be integrated to get past their opposition.

Caution #3: Remember that politics and business
  have different rules

Business executives, particularly those who sit at the top of hierarchical organizations, are used to telling folks what to do—and seeing it get done. The game is played by different rules in the political arena. Recall former Pittsburgh mayor Tom Murphy's description of the political realm as "more chaotic because it is democratic." Operating in the political sphere requires flexibility, tact, patience, the ability to listen to those with whom one disagrees vehemently as well as those who take your side, willingness to negotiate (and to compromise), and the thickest of skin. All of those things are important in business, too, but in the end the person at the top often has the authority to dictate the outcome. Not everyone in the company has a vote. Getting the facts right is critical, because the business executive caught in a mistake—or worse, a misrepresentation—loses credibility. And it goes without saying that a CEO whose company is dependent on government contracts or regulatory approval for its operation can frequently be neutralized if a political entity is disturbed by his or her actions. Such CEOs won't have much luck telling an elected official what to do.

One key to success in this political game is exhibiting a willingness to let others—in particular, the politicians—take the credit. Effective urban statesmen remember, as Rick Stafford has already reminded us, that politicians need to get credit for what they do—that's how they keep their jobs. Utah business executive Keith Rattie recalls how his 2015 Alliance colleague Scott Anderson capitalized on this trait through his talent for planting ideas: "He had a very low-key, self-effacing way of convincing the guy across the table that the change Scott was advocating was the other guy's idea."[9]

---

[9] Keith Rattie, interview, 9 April 2012.

Anderson would then remain behind the scenes; the politician got the publicity.

I observed this truth first-hand both in my early days with Research Atlanta and the Atlanta Action Forum (Bill Calloway was a master at working from the background) and with the Grady task force. With Grady, once the task force had made its recommendation, we had to wait until the Fulton-DeKalb Hospital Authority had "made it their own" to get action. The FDHA commissioned their own task force to study the work of our task force; their task-force results confirmed ours and gave them ownership of the proposal. When the negotiations over the content of the lease that would allow the new 501(c)(3) entity to manage the hospital began, we spent hours in meetings, changing wording and then changing it back again. This strategy allowed the hospital authority to maintain both control over the bricks and mortar through a lease agreement and its commitment to Grady's mission of service to indigent patients, even though the bones of the agreement were predetermined by the conditions that the Woodruff Foundation had placed on its $200 million gift. We went out of our way to congratulate the FDHA on their courage in adopting the new structure (especially in light of the opposition from the Grady Coalition and other community activists) and to give them credit for their willingness to make the change. It was clear to Pete Correll, Tom Bell, Michael Russell, and to me that it was more important that the change in governance take place than that the business community get all the credit.

Caution #4: Don't change the rules without both
  necessity and permission

Business leaders have limited time available to dedicate to public-policy issues. When one recruits these leaders to help in a public policy effort, it is important to be clear about the commitment expected from them in terms of time, effort, and resources. (As I've already noted, it is difficult for business executives to commit more than six to nine months to a project, and set beginning and end dates are pretty much a requirement.) It is equally important that that expectation not change without their consent. To justify such a change, one must both demonstrate necessity and get permission.

The contrasting experience of the leaders in two of our case studies is useful here. Houston's Disaster Planning and Recovery Task Force began its work with a mission of responding to a report by the Governor's Commission on Disaster Recovery and Renewal. At its initial meeting, the group agreed to expand its mission to include a needs assessment and planning process, as well as a series of "disaster avoidance initiatives" for the greater Houston region. [10] As they proceeded with constructing a response to the governor, the group also developed and distributed a survey to assess the impact of Hurricane Ike on the greater Houston business community. The group began its work on 12 February 2009 and issued its report to the governor on June 10—nine months after the hurricane, which hit 13 September 2008.

I've already discussed the loss of momentum this group experienced after their report was issued. I think this happened as a result of a change in the perception of the task-force members regarding the necessity and urgency of their work. Only a few Houston businesses took the time to respond to their survey, indicating a lack of current interest in the issues raised; the businesses seem to have moved on (whether or not they should have done so). Thereafter, the business executives on the task force (with a couple of exceptions) did the same. Recall our discussion of "tipping points" in the last chapter; at least some of those crucial questions ("What other concerns occupy the people who need to be engaged?"; "How deeply are people affected by the problem?"; "What are senior authority figures saying about the issue?") appeared to be getting answers other than "Let's work on the disaster task force!"

---

[10] Task Force mission statement provided by Elaine Barber.

By contrast, the Grady Task Force extended its mission for a select group of its members, with permission and by necessity, and followed through on the change to achieve success. The bulk of the task force committed to a ninety-day project, involving four meetings with some work between the gatherings. (We asked all the task-force members to tour the hospital, and there were a number of reports distributed with which they had to become familiar.) But once the final report was issued, the work of the journeyman task-force member was complete.

Such was not the case for our task-force leadership. Pete Correll, Tom Bell, and Michael Russell, along with me and several other Chamber staff (in particular, Senior Vice Presidents Renay Blumenthal and Esther Campi), continued to work on implementing the task-force recommendations. Our more typical task-force process is to develop recommendations and hand them over to an implementing authority. In the case of Grady, there was no one to take the ball. The FDHA had made it clear that, should we simply hand the recommendations to them, they would likely place our work in a drawer. As you've already heard from Tom Bell, that would have constituted failure for us. So this group undertook the task of following through, lobbying the county commissions and the hospital authority, visiting the private foundations in search of funding, and helping to negotiate the agreements to put the changes in place. This smaller group realized that without such an effort the recommendations of the task force would never be implemented (that's "necessity") so we agreed among ourselves to work until it was done (that's "permission").

I'm sure urban statesmen face other hazards, but these are the ones that have presented themselves most obviously to me, and none of these cautions suggests to me that business executives should avoid the demands of the public-policy arena.

CEOs have leadership and execution skills that can aid in the development and successful implementation of a wide range of public-policy solutions. The use of those skills can benefit all of us, in our capacities both as business people and as citizens, and they can benefit our communities as well. The late John W. Gardner, former Secretary of Health, Education, and Welfare and the founder of Common Cause, once wrote, "If we want to preserve the kind of society we have—a society in which a high proportion of the talent, resources, and institutional strengths lie outside government—we must find ways of mobilizing those assets on behalf of the community when occasion requires." [11] He argued for the banding together of leaders from business, government, and non-profit institutions into "networks of responsibility" designed to "appraise and seek to resolve the larger problems of their community, region, nation or world...."[12] Such public-private partnerships require the presence of business leaders committed to the public good as well as to the success of their business enterprises, and constitute the essential work of the urban statesman.

---

[11] John W. Gardner, *On Leadership* (New York: The Free Press, 1990) 102.
[12] Ibid., 107.

Acknowledgments

Book-writing and urban statesmanship have something in common: neither is something you do on your own.

This book grew out of a TED-X talk I gave in 2010 where I used the rescue of Atlanta's Grady Hospital as the basis for arguing that CEOs can and should serve as urban statesmen. The road from talk to book involved much work by many people, and I am grateful to all of them. Esther Campi, who was then the Metro Atlanta Chamber's Senior Vice President for Communications, helped me pull together my initial thoughts and sent me to Dr. Ken Bernhardt at Georgia State University's Robinson College of Business when I needed help with research. Ken, in turn, directed me to Laura Poe, who spent months researching other cities to identify and develop the case studies discussed here and arranging visits for me to meet some of the key leaders we identified. She has been relentless in fact-checking each story. I also appreciate greatly the willingness of Marc Jolley and Mercer University Press to take on the work of a fledgling author.

The staff of the Metro Atlanta Chamber, particularly Janice Rys, Hans Gant, and Renay Blumenthal, shared their contacts and wisdom with me as I worked to identify urban statesmen around the country. I deeply appreciate Richard Anderson, CEO of Delta Air Lines and chairman of the Metro Atlanta Chamber Board and the Chamber's Executive Committee for allowing me to use the Chamber's resources to work on this project.

My colleagues in chambers across the US shared with me stories of the urban statesmen at work in their cities and their thoughts on what made those people successful. I am particularly grateful to Roy Williams in Oklahoma City, Mike Gaymon in Columbus, Georgia, Lane Beattie in Salt Lake City, and Jeff Moseley, past president of the Great Houston Partnership, for sharing their urban statesmen with me. Other nationally known urban leaders also suggested possible case studies. They include Rick Stafford, former Allegheny Conference CEO; Rob Radcliff of Resource Development Group; Dick Fleming, past president of the Denver and St. Louis regional chambers; Bob McNulty, president of Partners for Livable Communities; and Mick Fleming, president of American Chamber of Commerce Executives.

And then there are the urban statesmen themselves. Over the years, I have observed many business executives operating in the public policy arena, and I have always been impressed by the difference these people made in their communities. The people I've written about in these studies are the best of the best. I'm proud to call Pete Correll, Michael Russell, and Tom Bell friends as well as extraordinary urban statesmen, and I've appreciated the chance to get to meet and/or learn about the work of the other folks described here: Ray Ackerman, Ron Norick, Scott Anderson, Mark Howell, Clark Ivory, Keith Rattie, Dr. Mae Jemison, and John Turner. They are all exceptional people who have made extraordinary contributions to their cities.

Finally, I have to admit I would never have been in a position to write any of this without the support of my assistant, Holly Swing, with whom I've worked for twenty-seven years, my wife Nancy, and my daughters Stephanie and Lindsay and their families. They've been there through thick and thin, good times and bad, and that's made all the difference.

My thanks to you all.

Bibliography

Alliance for Regional Stewardship. *Regional Stewardship: A Commitment to Place Monograph* 1. Palo Alto CA: Alliance for Regional Stewardship, 2000.

Bayor, Ronald H. *Race and the Shaping of Twentieth-Century Atlanta*. Chapel Hill: University of North Carolina Press, 1996.

Beattie, Lane. Address, Boise ID, 5 September 2007.

Blackburn, Bob L. *Heart of the Promised Land: Oklahoma County, An Illustrated Histor*. Woodland Hills CA: Windsor Publications, 1982).

Burke, Bob, with Joan Gilmore. *Old Man River: The Life of Ray Ackerman*. Oklahoma City: Oklahoma Heritage Association, 2002.

Conner, Daryl R. *Leading at the Edge of Chaos*. New York: John Wiley & Sons, 1998.

———. *Managing at the Speed of Change: How Resilient Managers Succeed and Prosper Where Others Fail*. New York: Villard Books, 1992.

Fleishman, Joel L. "The Real Against the Ideal—Making the Solution Fit the Problem: The Atlanta Public School Agreement of 1973." In *Roundtable Justice: Case Studies In Conflict Resolution—Reports to the Ford Foundation*. Edited by Robert B. Goldmann. Boulder CO: Westview Press, 1980.

Frey Foundation. "The New Landscape of Civic Business: How Business Leadership is Influencing Civic Progress in Our Metropolitan Regions Today," 2012.

———. "Taking Care of Civic Business: How Formal CEO-Level Business Leadership Groups Have Influenced Civic Progress in Key American Cities," March 1993.

FutureWorks. "Minding Their Civic Business: A Look at the New Ways Regional Business-Civic Organizations are Making a Difference in Metropolitan North America." Arlington, MA, 2004.

Gardner, John W. *On Leadership*. New York: The Free Press, 1990.

George, Bill. *7 Lessons for Leading in Crisis*. San Francisco: Jossey-Bass, 2009.

———. *True North: Discovering Your Authentic Leadership*. New York: John Wiley & Sons, 2007.

George Washington Institute of Public Policy. "Corporate Citizenship and Urban Problem Solving: The Changing Civic Role of Business Leaders in American Cities." Brookings Institution Metropolitan Policy Program, September 2006.

Gladwell, Malcolm. *The Tipping Point: How Little Things Can Make a Big Difference*. Boston: Little, Brown and Company, 2000.

———. "The Tipping Point." http://www.gladwell.com/tippingpoint (accessed 6 September 2012).

Governor's Commission for Disaster Recovery and Renewal (Texas). "Final Report to Governor Rick Perry." January 2010.

Grant, Adam. *Give and Take: The Hidden Social Dynamics of Success*. New York: Viking/The Penguin Group, 2013.

Greater Houston Partnership. "Recommendations to the Governor's Commission for Disaster Recovery and Renewal Report." 10 June 2009.

Grove, Andrew S. *Only the Paranoid Survive: How to Exploit the Crisis Points that Challenge Every Company and Career*. New York: Doubleday, 1996.

Heifetz, Ronald A., Alexander Grashow, and Marty Linsky. *The Practice of Adaptive Leadership: Tools and Tactics for Changing Your Organization and the World*. Boston: Harvard Business Press, 2009.

Heifetz, Ronald A., and Marty Linsky. *Leadership on the Line: Staying Alive Through the Dangers of Leading*. Boston: Harvard Business School Press, 2002.

Henton, Douglas, John Melville, and Kim Walesh. *Civic Revolutionaries: Igniting the Passion for Change in America's Communitie*. San Francisco: Jossey-Bass, 2004.

Hollender, Jeffrey, and Stephen Fenichell. *What Matters Most: How a Small Group of Pioneers Is Teaching Social Responsibility to Big Business, and Why Big Business is Listening*. New York: Basic Books, 2004.

Hsu, Jeremy. "100 Year Starship Project, Led by Ex-Astronaut Mae Jemison, Sets Sights on Distant Stars." *Innovation News Daily*, 21 May 2012. http://www.huffingtonpost.com/2012/05/21/100-year-starship-project-mae-jemison-stars_n_1908922.html (accessed 23 May 2012).

"In Receding Floodwaters, More Damage Found." MSNBC. http://www.msnbc.msn.com/id/9389157/ns/us_news-katrina_the_long_road_back/t/receding-floodwaters-more-damage-found/ (accessed 21 May 2012).

Jemison, Mae. *Find Where the Wind Goes: Moments from my Life*. New York: Scholastic Press, 2001.

Keating, Larry. *Atlanta: Race, Class, and Urban Expansion*. Philadelphia: Temple University Press, 2001.

Kotter, John P. *Leading Change*. Boston: Harvard Business School Press, 1996.

Kotter, John P., and Dan S. Cohen. *The Heart of Change: Real-Life Stories of How People Change Their Organizations*. Boston: Harvard Business School Press, 2002.

Kruse, Kevin M. *White Flight: Atlanta and the Making of Modern Conservatism.* Princeton NJ: Princeton University Press, 2005.

Lackmeyer, Steve, and Jack Money. *OKC: Second Time Around.* Oklahoma City: Full Circle Press, 2006.

Metro Atlanta Chamber, Greater Grady Task Force papers (private collection) January 2007—May 2008.

"Mission Statement: Disaster Recovery and Planning Task Force." Provided by Elaine Barber, Vice President for Public Policy, Greater Houston Partnership.

Research Atlanta. "School Desegregation in Metro Atlanta 1954–1973." Atlanta: Atlanta Research, Inc., February 1973.

Rosenberg, Brett. "Oklahoma City: A Win-Win." *U.S. Mayor Newspaper*, 28 June2010. http://usmayors.org/usmayornewspaper/documents/06_28_10/pg21_OKC_win_win.asp (accessed on 10 October 2011).

Stone, Clarence N. *Regime Politics: Governing Atlanta 1946–1988.* Lawrence: University Press of Kansas, 1989.

Trotter, Michael. "Michael H. Trotter Papers." Y001, Social Change Collection, Special Collections and Archives, Georgia State University, Atlanta, Georgia.

———. "Research Atlanta: The Early Days." (Unpublished paper) Research Atlanta: 1987.

Utah 2015 Transportation Alliance. "Accelerating Utah Transportation Investments: Needs, Costs, Funding Options," 12 June 2006.

Newspapers
Atlanta Journal/ Atlanta Constitution/ Atlanta Journal-Constitution
The Columbus Ledger-Enquirer
The Daily Oklahoman/the Oklahoman
Deseret News
Houston Chronicle
New York Times
Salt Lake City Tribune
Tulsa World
Wall Street Journal

Interviews
Atlanta
Tom Bell
Esther Campi

Pete Correll
Michael Russell
Che Watkins

Oklahoma City
Andy Burke
Charles Van Rysselberge
Roy Williams

Salt Lake City
Mike Allegra
Scott Anderson
Lane Beattie
Bruce Bingham
Carlos Braceros
Ron Clegg
Natalie Gochnour
Dave Golden
Andrew Gruber
Bob Henrie
Mark Howell
Clark Ivory
Scott Parson
Keith Rattie
LaVarr Webb

Houston
Joni Baird
Elaine Barber
Mae Jemison
Jeff Moseley
Francisco Sanchez

Columbus
Jimmy Blanchard
Gardiner W. Garrard
Mike Gaymon
Tom Helton
Tim Mescon
Kessel Stelling

Mat Swift
John Turner
Williams B. Turner
Jimmy Yancey

Others
Andy Burke
Tom DiFiore
Brian Ferguson
Mick Fleming
Maureen McDonald
Bob McNulty
Tom Murphy
Rob Radcliff
Rick Stafford
Otis White

Index

2015 Alliance 71-84, 137, 145, 152, 156, 161-162, 164; Action plan 161-162; Collaborative effort 83-84; Commissioned transportation study 71, 141, 152; Decision to include both roads and transit 72, 141, 149; Funding mechanisms 74-76; Goal 71, 161; Implementation 83-84, 156; Media scrutiny 164; Messaging strategy 72, 81, 145; Public support for proposal 78, 81-82; Sales tax proposal 74-76; Scope and timetables 156; Special legislative session 76-80, 137, 149; Study recommendations 72-73; Use of Chamber as base 73, 81, 152

Ackerman, Ray 24, 31-46, 139, 143, 146; And the North Canadian River 34; As a visionary 34, 36, 44-45, 139; Chamber of Commerce retreat 1990 33-34; Oklahoma River 44; Rowing facility 44

Aflac 105, 117, 119, 129, 149; And downtown Columbus redevelopment 105; Financial commitment 117, 119, 149

Alabama Rivers Alliance 108

Alden Labs 115; Chattahoochee River model 115

Alexander Contracting 121

Allegheny Conference ii, 67

Allen, Ivan, Jr. 1-2, 4

Alvarez and Marsal 54, 151

Anderson, John 108-109, 114, 118, 128,145,150; Design of Columbus whitewater course 114, 150; Evaluation of dams 108-109; Official project announcement 118; Olympic whitewater course designer 108; Recommendation to use the river bed as whitewater course 108-109

Anderson, Scott 24, 28, 69-84, 139-140, 141, 176; Effectiveness with legislators 80, 176; Special session support 79

Army Corps of Engineers 35, 44, 100, 109, 110-111, 114, 116, 119, 121, 128, 129, 138, 143, 150-151, 158; And cost estimates 116; And North Canadian River 35, 44; And river restoration funding 109, 119, 128, 129; Approval process 110-111, 121; Environmental impact of whitewater project 109, 128, 129, 150-151; Feasibility study 110; Intervening priorities 110-111; Permits 120-121

Arrington, David 118

Atlanta Action Forum 2-13, 177; And MARTA 5-6; And Research Atlanta 2-11; And school desegregation 6-11; As a "joint voice" for business 3-4; "Compromise of 1973" 10-11; Other issues 12-13

Atlanta Urban Corps 2

Babin, Anna 90; Task Force role 90

Baird, Joni 90, 92, 96, 97, 98, 136, 139, 146; Group management skills of leader 98; Need for communications network 92, 97; Task Force role 90

Barber, Elaine 86-87, 89, 90-91, 96, 146, 167; Absence of media coverage 167; Group management skills of leader 90, 96; Recruiting the task force 86-87; Task Force mission 89

Batson-Cook Construction 121, 122

Be transparent 163-167; Creating credibility and trust 163-164; Media scrutiny 164

Beasley, Joe 56, 58, 64

Beattie, Lane 24, 69-84, 139-140; Business community control of project 83-84; Value of collaboration 83-84; Importance of balanced message 72; Special session support 79

Becker, Mayor Ralph 83

Bell, Judge Griffin 2, 8

Bell, Tom 22, 24, 26, 28, 47-68, 136, 137, 140, 143, 144, 147, 157, 167, 170, 177, 179; And controversy 170; And Emory University Hospital board 48, 65, 147; And Fulton-DeKalb Hospital Authority 52, 65, 147; And implementation of recommendations 60, 157, 179; As a "detail man" 65; Political contacts 65

Berry, George 1-2

Best Practices 133-169; Be transparent with the public and the press 163-167; Create a clear, simple action plan 159-163; Define your mission, scope of work, and timeline 154-159; Do your homework 149-154

Find a forum 142-146; Get invited in 146-149; Play to your strengths 139-142; Select a tipping point issue 133-138

Bibb Dam 129

Bishop, Richard 116, 118, 121, 123, 125, 165; Announcement of contractors 121; Announcement of outfitters 123; Official whitewater project announcement 118

Blanchard, Jimmy 99, 105

Blumenthal, Renay 53, 54, 179

Borders, Lisa 52, 57-58, 64

Bradley-Turner Foundation 100, 104, 108, 119, 128, 145, 149; Funding for dam purchase 112, 119, 149

Breaching the dams 116, 120, 122-123, 124; City Mills Dam 124; Cost 116; Eagle and Phenix Dam 122-123

Bricktown Canal 43-33

Burdeshaw, Ed 118

Burke, Andy 174

Butler, Steve 118

Calhoun v. Cook 7

Calloway, W.L. 3, 4, 6, 12, 177

Campi, Esther 53, 59, 145-146, 167, 179

Cautionary tales 170-180; Avoid conflicts of interest 170-173; Business and politics have different rules 176-177; Change rules only with necessity and permission 177-179; Watch out for turf protectors 173-176

Cavezza, Carmen 118

CEOs and ; Big picture 23; Boundary crossing 24-26, 27; Community involvement as a cultural value 19-22, 171-172; Consolidation and relocation 20-21

Crisis management 27-29 ; Dealing with controversy 17-18, 170-171; Doing good while doing well 16-18; Globalization 20-22; Leadership organizations 14, 23, 172; Political acumen 26-27; Quality of life issues 23;

Restructuring 20; Sense of place 18-24; Sharing the credit 25-26, 176-177; Team-building 29-30; Tipping points 27-28, 133-138 Visionary pragmatism 23; Working through business/civic organizations 14-15, 142-146

Chattahoochee Fall Line Alliance 101, 107, 108, 109, 110, 111-115, 117, 130, 145, 148, 150-151, 158, 165; And information collection 150-151; And purchase of dams 111-112; As ad hoc committee of Uptown Columbus 107, 145; Composition 108; Decision criteria 111-115; Decision to proceed 117, 148; Fundraising 117; And media scrutiny 130, 165; River studies and surveys 114; Timelines 158; Use of forums 145

Chattahoochee River 100, 108-109, 113, 114-115, 125; Early vision for whitewater channel 108; Impact of power generation on river volume 115; Public support for whitewater project 113; Removing historic dams 108-109; Studies and surveys 114

Chattahoochee Riverkeeper 108, 113, 128, 145; Endorsement of river restoration project 113

Chattahoochee River Restoration Project 99-132, 137-138, 158, 159; Appealing to diverse interests 129; Broad-based support for 113, 137-138; Composition of official committee 117-118; Contractors 121, 122-123; Decommissioning the dams 120-121, 159; Fundraising 119-120; Groundbreaking 121; Implementation structure 118;

Opening Day 124-126; Permits 120-121, 159; Project announcement 118; Project cost 115-116; Project description 100; Ready2Raft 118, 158; Results 130-132

City Mills Dam 102, 108, 111, 116, 118, 124, 129, 160; Breaching the dam 124; Purchasing the dam 111-112

Civic involvement 18-24, 170-173; And corporate culture 22-23, 171-172

Coffee, Glen 109-110, 128; And feasibility study 109-110

Columbus, Georgia 99-132, 148, 149, 160; Chattahoochee River dams at 101-102; City/county government 108; Downtown decline 102-103; Downtown redevelopment 104-106, 131-132, 148; Economy 101; History 101; Involvement of business community 99-100, 105, 106, 117; Riverwalk 105-106; Uniqueness of whitewater venue 116-117

Columbus Council 109-110, 117, 119, 123, 124, 129, 138, 145, 149, 158, 165; As sponsor for feasibility study 109-110, 145, 165; Financial commitment 117, 119, 149

Columbus State University 106, 116, 118, 120, 131-132; Economic analysis of river restoration project 116, 118, 120; Promoting Whitewater 131-132

Concerned Black Clergy 57, 58, 64, 166, 175

Conflicts of interest 170-173; And level of civic involvement 171-172; Dealing with controversial issues 170-171

Correll, A.D. (Pete) 13, 17-18, 24,
47-68, 137, 140, 143, 144, 145-
146, 147, 157, 159-160, 166-167,
170, 175, 177, 179; And action
plan 159-160; And conflict of
interest 17-18, 66, 170; And
controversy 170; And Emory
University Hospital board 47-48;
And Fulton-DeKalb Hospital
Authority 52, 147; And
implementation of
recommendations 157, 179; And
Jimmy Williams 61, 66; And
racial issues 57, 58-60, 166, 175;
As "spear-catcher" 66
Court of Appeals, Fifth Circuit 8
Create an action plan 159-163; And
Columbus, Georgia 160-161;
And Grady Hospital 159-160;
And Houston 162-163; And
MAPS 161
And Salt Lake City 161-162; Value
of simplicity 159, 163
Dedwylder, Rozier 103, 104
Define mission, scope and timeline
154-159, 177; Set specific
expectations 154-155; With
ballot initiatives and legislation
155-156
DeKalb County Commission 50, 53,
61, 62, 63, 136, 147
Deloitte Consulting 53, 151
DiFiore, Tom 23, 24, 27
Disaster Planning and Recovery Task
Force (Greater Houston
Partnership) 85-98, 135, 139,
143, 146, 153-154, 157-158, 162-
163, 167, 178; Action plan 162-
163; Composition 88-89;
Information gathering 153-154;
Issues 92-96; Lack of press
coverage 154, 167; Loss of
momentum 96-97, 158, 178; Loss
of support staff 97, 146

Mission 89, 178; Organization 90-91;
Process 90-91, 95, 157;
Recommendations 92-96; Scope
and timelines 157-158
Do your homework 149-154;
Importance of good information
149-150; Knowledge of political
constituencies and 154; Sources
of information 150
Eagle and Phenix Dam 102, 106, 109,
111-112, 118, 122-123, 124, 130,
160; Breaching the dam 122-123;
Purchasing the dam 111-112
Eastman Chemical Company 173
Eaves, John 52
Edwards, Dr. Chris 52, 65, 147
Emory Healthcare Board 48, 65, 147
Fall line 101,102, 122
Federal Energy Regulatory
Commission 100, 120;
Decommissioning the dams 120
Ferguson, Brian 173.175
Find a forum 142-146; And
credibility 143-144; And Grady
Memorial Hospital 49-53; And
media 145-146; Business/civic
organizations and 142;
Information and logistical
support 142, 144-145; Selecting a
forum 143
Fleming, Mick 17, 19-20
Fort, Vincent 56, 58, 64, 175
Frankfurt Short Bruza 38, 152
Franklin, Mayor Shirley 13, 52, 64
Fulton County Commission 50, 52,
53, 61, 62, 63, 136, 147
Fulton-DeKalb Hospital Authority
50, 52, 60-61, 62, 63, 65, 136,
147, 151-152, 165, 177, 179; And
implementation of
recommendations 62, 177, 179
Gardner, Kem 71, 72
Garrard, Gardiner 99
Gaymon, Mike 99, 118

Georgia Hospital Association 54, 151
Georgia Power Company 108, 124, 125, 151
Georgia Institute of Technology (Georgia Tech) 1
Georgia State University Health Policy Center 54, 151
Get invited in 146-149; And Greater Grady Task Force 50, 52, 147-148; And turf protection 173-176; Ballot initiative as invitation 149; Direct invitation (Houston) 148; Versus meddling 146-147
Gilbert, Dan 125, 130
Gochnour, Natalie 73, 80, 84, 137, 145; And media 145; Sense of urgency 73; Special session support 80
Good Government Atlanta 2
Governor's Commission for Disaster Recovery and Renewal 86, 162-163
Grady Coalition 56, 57, 164, 165, 166, 175
Grady Memorial Hospital 47-68, 134; Financial issues 48, 50-52, 53, 54, 55, 61-62, 66; Governance structure 50-52, 55, 62, 63, 66; History 50-53; Impact of closing on medical care 51-52, 53; Treating patients from other counties, financial impact 51, 54
Grady Memorial Hospital Corporation 62, 63, 67; Board of Directors 63, 67; Relationship with FDHA 62
Greater Columbus Chamber of Commerce 105, 108, 113, 118, 128, 142, 145; Endorsement of river restoration project 113, 145
Greater Grady Task Force 52-68, 141, 145-146, 151-152, 157, 159-160, 165-167, 175-176, 177, 179; And 501c3 action plan 55, 62, 66,

159-160, 165-167, 177, 179; And information collection 151-152; And the media 58-60, 63, 145-146, 152, 165-167; Creation of 52-53; Composition of 52-53, 57, 64; Implementation of recommendations 60, 141, 157, 177, 179; Racial issues 56-60, 141, 165-167, 175-176; Recommendations 55-56; Scope and timetable 157; Transparency 58-59, 166-167
Greater Houston Partnership 85-98, 142, 148; Appointment of Disaster Planning and Recovery Task Force 85-86; As a supportive forum 142; Composition 88
Greater Salt Lake City Chamber of Commerce 69-84, 142, 152; As a supportive forum 142; Fund-raising for media campaign 81; Transportation funding proposal 74-80
Harris County, Texas 88
Haupert, John 67
Hill, Jesse 5-6
Historic Columbus Foundation 108, 113, 145; And preservation of dam structures 113; Endorsement of river restoration project 113, 145
Howell, Mark 73, 84, 139-140
Horrow, Rick 37, 144, 146, 152
HTNB Corporation 71, 152
Huntsman, Governor Jon, Jr. 76-80; Income tax proposal 78-79
Hurricane Ike 2008 88, 148, 167, 178
"Ike Dike" 94-96
Ivory, Clark 24, 69, 73, 84, 139-140, 143-144, 145
Jackson, Maynard 4, 12, 13
Jemison, Dr. Mae 85-98, 139, 141, 146, 148, 153-154, 155;

Appointment to Disaster Planning and Recovery Task Force 85-86, 148; Biographical information 85; Composing the task force 86, 88-89; Group management skills 90, 139

Management of controversy 95-96; Reasons for selection as task force chair 86; Setting expectations 155; Task force mission 89; Task Force process 90-91, 95, 153-154

Jones, Charles G. "Gristmill" 35

Jones, Vernon 52, 61, 147

Killpack, Utah State Senator Sheldon 77

King, Lonnie 3, 8, 9, 10-11

Lane, Mills B. 3, 21

Lindsay, John, mayor of New York City 1, 2

Loss of momentum (Houston) 96-97, 157-158, 178

Lowery, Rev. Joseph 58, 166

MAPS 38-46, 135, 139, 141, 144, 146, 149, 156, 161, 164-165; Action plan 39-40, 161; Aftermath 44-45, 141

As a model project 46; Implementation 42-44; Media scrutiny 164-165; Opinion polling 39-41, 152, 156; Strategic decisions 39-41, 141, 144, 156

Marshall, Ron 56

Mays, Dr. Benjamin 10

McDonald, Maureen 16, 24

McDonald, Rev. Tim 57, 59-60, 64, 68, 165-166, 175

McLaughlin, Rick 108-109, 114-115, 128, 145, 150; Design of Columbus whitewater course 114-115, 150; Evaluation of dams 108-109; Olympic whitewater course designer 108; Recommendation to use the river

bed as whitewater course 108-109

McNulty Robert (Bob) 22, 28

Merrell, Dr. William 94, 97

Mescon, Dr. Tim 99, 132

Metro Atlanta Chamber 49-68, 136, 142, 143, 144, 145-146, 147-148, 175; Appointment of Greater Grady Task Force 53; As forum for task force 49, 67, 143,144,145; Decision to engage with Grady Hospital 49-50, 52; Grady Health Foundation award 68; Invitation to intervene 52-53, 147-148

Moseley, Jeff 86, 98, 148; On Gov. Perry's staff 86, 148; Selection of Jemison as task force chair 86

Mountainland Association of Governments 70

Murphy, Tom 26, 176

NAACP 7-11

Nantahala Outdoor Center 123-124

National Oceanic and Atmospheric Administration 119, 129; Financial contribution 119

Norick, Ron 31-46, 139, 145, 149, 156, 164; And media scrutiny 38, 164; And Metro Area Projects Task Force 37; And scope of project 156; Approval strategy 39-41; As project implementer 42-44, 45, 139, 156

North Canadian River 31, 34-36

North Highland Dam 101, 116, 124, 130

Oklahoma City 31-46; Chamber of Commerce 33, 34, 36, 37, 41, 45, 142, 146, 152; Negative image 31-34

Oklahoma City Ditch and Water Power Company 35

Oklahoma City Riverfront Redevelopment Authority 35, 36

Oklahoma River 44
Open-mindedness 141
Organizing students 1-2
Overholser, Henry 35
Parson, Scott 73, 81, 84, 139-140
Pei, I.M. 36
Perry, Governor Rick 86, 148;
    Commission for Disaster
    Recovery and Renewal 86, 162-
    163
Phenix City, Alabama 100, 108, 119,
    123, 124, 129, 132, 160; And
    funding for dam purchase 112,
    119
Phillips, Jim 128
Playing to your strengths 139-142;
    Ackerman, Ray 139, 141;
    Anderson, Scott 139-140, 141;
    Beattie, Lane 139-140, 141 ;
    Bell, Tom 140, 141; Correll, Pete
    140, 141; Howell, Mark 139-140
Ivory, Clark 139-140; Jemison, Dr.
    Mae 139, 141; Norick, Ron 139;
    Open-mindedness 141; Parson,
    Scott 139-140; Rattie, Keith 139-
    140; Right people in charge 139;
    Russell, Michael 140, 141
Taking the long view 141; Turner,
    John 140, 141
Political acumen 26-27, 154
Portman, John 3, 21
Proposition 3 80-82; Election result
    82; Endorsements 82
Public/private partnerships 14-15, 26-
    27, 92, 97-98, 180
Purchasing the dams 111-112
Radcliff, Rob 16, 17
Rattie, Keith 18, 24, 69, 79, 81-82,
    84, 139-140, 143, 152, 171, 176;
    And controversy 171; Endorses
    Huntsman tax proposal 79;
    Funding-raising strategy for
    media campaign 81 ; Reasons for
    broad-based support 81-82

Ready2Raft 118, 158; Scope and
    timelines 158
Regional Alliance for Economic
    Development (Tennessee) 173-
    174
Research Atlanta 2-11, 177; And
    school desegregation 6-11
Ripe issues 134-135, 178
Riverwalk 105-106, 117; And
    combined sewer overflow
    construction 105-106
Rules of politics 25-26, 176; And
    giving others credit 25-26, 176
Russell, Michael 24, 52-68. 137, 140,
    143, 144, 157, 165, 167, 177,
    179; And controversy 170; And
    implementation of
    recommendations 157, 179; As
    ambassador to the African-
    American community 64-65,
    165; Leadership style 64;
    Meeting with Concerned Black
    Clergy 57-58, 64, 175
Salt Lake County Council 74-76, 77,
    78, 162; And special legislative
    session 77; Sales tax preference
    74-76; UTA funding request 74
Salt Lake County transportation
    issues 69-84, 135, 149, 161-162,
    164; Action plan 161-162;
    Approval by special legislative
    session 80; And regional
    planning agencies 70; Funding
    proposals 74-76; Improvements
    prior to 2002 Olympics 70
Invitation to participate 149;
    Initiatives by competing cities
    70; Media scrutiny 164; Study
    results 71-72
Sanchez, Francisco 88-92, 96, 97, 98,
    136, 158; Need for
    communications network 92, 97;
    Harris County, Texas, statistics
    88; Loss of momentum 158;

Management of controversy 96;
Public-private partnerships 92,
97; Task Force mission 89-90,
98; Task Force process 91
Scott Bridge Company 121
Smith, Frank 8, 9
Smith , Joseph (Joe) 107, 128
Special Session, Utah legislature 76-
80; 2006 legislative session 76
Stafford, Rick 25-26, 67-68, 142,
150, 176; Giving politicians
credit 25-26, 176; Importance of
good information 150; Role of
business/civic organizations 67-
68, 142
Stelling, Kessel 99
Stephenson, Pam 52, 63, 65, 147
Stewardship of authority 27
Stewardship of place 18
Story, Otis 63
Swift, Mat 99, 105, 111-112, 113,
118, 120, 127, 136; And
fundraising strategy 120; And
implementation committee 118;
And purchase of dams 111-112
Synovus 105, 106; And downtown
Columbus redevelopment 105-
106
Taking the long view 141
Texas hurricanes 86, 87-88;
Evacuation planning 87-88
"The Atlanta Way" 12, 56, 64
Thomas Keilhorn and Associates 38,
152
Time commitments 154-155, 177-
179
Timeline 154-159, 177-179
Tipping point 27-29, 133-138, 178;
And Columbus Georgia
whitewater project 136, 137-138;
And Grady Hospital 134, 136-
137; And Houston Task Force
135, 178; And media 135, 136-
137, 138; And Oklahoma City

MAPS 135; And Salt Lake City
referendum 135, 137; And
urgency 134-135, 137; "Burning
platform" 134; Costs versus
benefits 134-135; Defined 27-29,
133-134; Key questions 135;
Ripe issue 134; "Widespread"
urgency 136
Tom Warne and Associates 71, 152
Tomlinson, Mayor Teresa 121
Total Systems (TSYS) 105, 106, 117,
119-120, 128, 129, 149; And
downtown Columbus
redevelopment 105-106;
Financial commitment 117, 119,
149; Whitewater project and
employee recruitment 119-120
Transparency 163-167
Transportation funding options
(Utah) 74-80; Ballot authority
75-76; Bond issue/property tax
(UTA) 74
Incremental sales tax (Alliance
/Chamber proposal) 74;
Proposals compared 74-75
Tri-cities, Tennessee 173-175
Tri-cities Business Alliance 173
Trotter, Michael 2-3, 5
Trust for Public Lands 112; And
funding for dam purchase 112
Turf protectors 173-176
Turner, Billy 118, 121, 159, 165
Turner, John 99-132, 136, 140, 141,
143, 148-149, 150-151, 158-159,
160-161, 165; And action plan
160-161; And Army Corps of
Engineers 109, 110-111, 121,
128-129,143, 150-151, 158; And
Columbus culture 148-149; And
future development 130-132;
And historic preservation of dam
structures 113; And
implementation committee 118;
And information collection 111,

114, 141, 150-151; And media
scrutiny 126, 130, 165; And
model of Chattahoochee riverbed
115; And speed of process 110;
Appealing to diverse interests
129; As urban statesman 127-
130; Breaching the dams 123;
"Conversation not a sales pitch"
111, 127-128, 158
Fundraising strategy 117, 119-120,
129-130; Official project
announcement 118; Opening Day
124-126; Permits 120-121;
Problem-solving 128-129;
Quality of life issues 107, 119-
120, 129-130, 160-161; Scope
and timelines 158-159; Use of
experts 128; Vision for the river
106-110, 127
Turner, William B. 100, 103-104,
106, 107, 132; And W.C. Bradley
Company 103-104; And
Riverwalk 106
Uptown Columbus 105, 107, 111-
112, 113, 114, 118, 123, 142,
143, 158, 165; And media 165
And purchase of dams 111-112, 158;
As a supportive forum 142; As
whitewater park manager 123;
Cost-benefit analysis 116;
Decision to proceed 117;
Endorsement of river restoration
project 113; Opening Day 124-
126; Outfitters 123-124;
Timelines 158; Wave-shaper 124
USA Today "Built to Thrill" list 130
U.S. Fish and Wildlife Service 100,
108
Urban statesman, defined i-ii, 15,
168
Utah Department of Transportation
71, 73, 143, 152
Utah Foundation study 74-75

Utah Transit Authority 71, 73, 74,
143, 149, 152
Van Landingham, William 8-9
W.C. Bradley Company 100, 103-
104, 111, 117, 119, 127, 129,
132, 149; Financial commitment
117, 119, 149
Wasatch Front Range Council 70, 71-
72
Watkins, Che 53, 57-58, 146
Wade, Lyndon 9
Waterworth, Leonard 90, 94-96
"Ike Dike" 94-96; Task Force role 90
Wave-shaper 124
White, Otis 29, 103, 104, 106, 139
"Whitewater" 100, 113, 118, 125-
126, 132; Opening day 125-126;
Public support for 113; Project
announcement 118
Whitewater Express 123, 125, 130;
First season statistics 130;
Opening Day 125; You-Tube
video 130
Wickham, Neal 107, 128, 143
Williams, Jimmy 61, 66
Williams, Roy 19, 34
Woodruff Foundation 61, 66, 177
Yancey, Jimmy 99
Young, Michael 67